the **main**

the **main**
{recipes}

ANTHONY   SEDLAK

whitecap

Whitecap Books is known for its expertise in the cookbook market, and has produced some of the most innovative and familiar titles found in kitchens across North America. Visit our website at www.whitecap.ca.

Design by Mauve Pagé
Photography by David Bagosy (www.davidbagosy.com)
except photo on page 2 (bottom right) by Anthony Sedlak
Digital photo retouching by Alison Vieira (www.alisonvieira.com)
Story editing by Claire Leila Philipson
Recipe development by Claudia Bianchi
Recipe editing by Taryn Boyd
Proofread by Paula Ayer
Index by Carol Hamill

Printed in Canada by Friesens.

Library and Archives Canada Cataloguing in Publication

Sedlak, Anthony, 1983–
The main : recipes / Anthony Sedlak.

Includes index.
ISBN 978-1-55285-945-2

1. Cookery. I. Title.

TX714.S42 2008   641.5   C2008-902145-2

The publisher acknowledges the financial support of the Government of Canada through the Book Publishing Industry Development Program (BPIDP) and the Province of British Columbia through the Book Publishing Tax Credit.

08 09 10 11 12   5 4 3 2 1

For you, little Sophie—forever and always
my best friend and lover, and the sweetest of hearts

TABLE OF CONTENTS

INTRODUCTION

If you had told me over a decade ago—when I was a little 13-year-old punk—that someday I'd be writing an introduction to my book, I wouldn't have bought it. But that's how old I was when it all kicked off.

MY STORY

I grew up just a hop, skip, and a jump away from the base of Grouse Mountain (in North Vancouver, BC), where a red gondola whisks awaiting winter sporting enthusiasts up to a picturesque wonderland. Although I'd been an avid snowboarder since age 11, my parents were not about to drop the 600 beans necessary to get me a season's pass. It just wasn't going to happen. Instead, my mom, a master of exploring other avenues, took note of a classified ad in our local paper: the resort cafeteria at Grouse Mountain was hiring people to bus tables.

I was familiar with the café. It was a gong show in the winter, crammed with overly hyper, under-supervised young whippersnappers—just like me. Of course, a substantial amount of the appeal in going up the mountain was the fact that you were up there with just your mates—3,700 feet above the supervision of your parents.

I also knew full well that getting a job at the mountain meant a free season's pass. So I welcomed the opportunity. The fact that I was not yet of legal age to work didn't cross my mind, nor apparently the mind of the supervisor who hired me. I thought having a job was tops, not only for the regular paycheques that blew any average kid's allowance out of the water, but also because of the environment. My co-workers were older teens who were all notably cool. And the occasional after-shift beer would find its way to me. People treated me like a little brother—they looked out for me, taught me the ins and outs of the job, and occasionally put me in my place.

I had a positive attitude and a good work ethic. I enjoyed what I was doing, and I smiled at the right people. By 14, I was awarded "employee of the month." The owner, Mr. McLaughlin (I call him Stuart now), gave me a gift certificate to have dinner at the resort's flagship eatery. I couldn't get the guts to invite a girl for dinner, so I brought my best buddy at the time, Bryan Kelly. We ironed our khakis and polo shirts, and buffed up our best skateboarding shoes.

This was a turning point. To this day I don't remember what we ordered—most likely because at the time I didn't even know what I was ordering. I wasn't particularly well versed in

French culinary terms, and the food was a far cry from what I was used to or had ever experienced. Now, I don't know if I was sold on a culinary career right there and then, but I was definitely blown away by our meal. I was amazed to think that raw ingredients could be transformed and manipulated into something so refined and perfect.

From then on I pursued cooking both in high school, where I opted out of regular academics and instead chased down a culinary program, and at the mountain, where I was being whisked through the various kitchens. With its three restaurants, Grouse Mountain was the perfect platform from which to launch my culinary career; each restaurant provided me with a new set of challenges. Throughout my 11 years there, I always shared a kitchen with a great team, including several chefs who were genuinely proud of their profession and committed enough to mentor me.

After pursuing my Red Seal certification, I headed to London, England, and joined the kitchen of the renowned La Trompette restaurant in West London. After 16 months on the London culinary scene, I returned home to North Vancouver and accepted a chef position at The Observatory, Grouse Mountain's newly renovated high-end dining room.

During my time at The Observatory I won a series of culinary competitions in Vancouver. I was chosen as Canada's sole representative to compete in the Hans Bueschkens World Junior Chefs Challenge in Auckland, New Zealand—a once-in-a-lifetime opportunity. Doors were beginning to open, and my passion for cooking was becoming more and more serious. Later that year, I was one of six participants selected from across the country to compete in Food Network's Superstar Chef Challenge II, which I was lucky enough to win. I then went on to help develop and host Food Network's new TV series *The Main*.

I love that the network has something for everyone, from the novice to the seasoned home cook right through to the professional chef. Even some of my tightest friends, who are just regular guys in university (and who can't cook to save their lives), thoroughly enjoy watching Gordon Ramsay tear up some wannabe pro—I do too. I'm proud to be part of this family of hugely talented chefs and entertainers.

Sometimes I really feel like I won the lottery. I've had the chance to travel and meet some top chefs, and made some lifelong friends, all while cooking up a storm—the very thing I live for. If this turns out to be just a dream, well, don't wake me up!

MY PHILOSOPHY

As much as food is a social activity and something to be shared, it can also be very personal. Food and cooking has always been a part of me. This collection reflects not only who I am as a chef, both in the restaurant and at home, but also me as a person.

At the same time, every chef is a reflection of his or her mentors. Yes, I have logged countless unpaid hours, and have been dedicated, driven, hard-working, and all that. The truth is, many cooks and chefs are. But mostly I'm here today because I've always been surrounded by talented, passionate people who share my goals and aspirations. To those who have inspired and influenced me, as both a chef and a human being—thank you. You know who you are.

MY BOOK

The number one question I'm asked as a chef is: what is your favourite dish? I often reply that answering such a question would be like declaring your all-time favourite song. There are simply too many to name just one. So I like to think of this book as an album, a collection of my very favourite ingredients, dishes, and culinary experiences.

My goal with each recipe was to be true to my style: tasty, simple, and rustic fare presented elegantly.

But even the best of cookbooks are just guides, I want you to push your epicurean boundaries by exploring and experimenting with what's in this book. Take these recipes as guidelines, read about ingredients, learn some of my tools. (Check out the "Timing Is Everything" notes so that your dishes come together simultaneously.) Your natural accent and style will be apparent as you make the recipes and they will become, in a sense, yours. This is how all good chefs learn and how they eventually develop a repertoire of their own recipes and techniques.

Happy cooking. I hope this collection brings you the same joy I've experienced in creating it. And, oh yes—that's a main.

3

AGED CHEDDAR

Originating from the English town of Cheddar, cheddar cheese is now produced all over the world in countries including Canada, the United States, South Africa, Australia, and New Zealand. Traditional English cheddar is white and tastes sharp, pungent, and slightly earthy. Today, some mainstream producers in Canada and the United

States add a vegetable dye to cheddar to give it a distinct bright orange colour. This not only makes the cheese stand out, it also ensures a consistent colour from batch to batch.

It's rather sad that cheddar cheese has no legally protected designation of origin or methods of production. Because of this, cheddar has been

AGED CHEDDAR GRILLED CHEESE · CARAMELIZED ONION RELISH · HERBED MUSTARD DIP · CLASSIC FRENCH ONION SOUP

At any given point during my childhood there was undoubtedly a very large brick of bright-orange medium cheddar cheese in the fridge. I can't say I ran home early from school to indulge, but I did enjoy orange cheddar in many different ways, the ultimate being a grilled cheese sandwich. Today, the principle hasn't changed, but the ingredients have. My updated grilled cheese combines egg bread, salty aged cheddar, sweet pear, and my savoury Caramelized Onion Relish, all pan-fried to perfection in an egg-and-buttermilk mixture, which gives the sandwich a wonderfully tender crust.

When I was growing up, ketchup was like the nectar of the gods and eating a grilled cheese without it was unheard of. I still love a great tomato gastrique (ketchup), but my Herbed Mustard Dip brings the perfect bite to this sandwich. The grainy mustard mellows out the Dijon and gives the dip a nice texture. French onion soup, both a classic and a favourite of mine, also complements the sandwich perfectly. It's simple to prepare and has a great depth of flavour. The sweetness of both the onions and sherry provides a great contrast to the soup's aged cheddar topping. *{Serves 4}*

AGED CHEDDAR GRILLED CHEESE

8 slices challah (or other
  egg-based bread)
4 Tbsp Caramelized Onion Relish
2 Bosc pears, peeled and
  thinly sliced
4 slices aged cheddar cheese,
  cut ⅛ inch thick
2 Tbsp chopped thyme
salt and pepper
3 eggs
½ cup buttermilk
2 Tbsp butter

Preheat oven to 400°F.

On a work surface, lay out 4 slices of bread. Spread 1 Tbsp Caramelized Onion Relish on each. Top with sliced pears and cheddar cheese. Sprinkle each sandwich with thyme and salt and pepper. Top with remaining 4 slices of bread.

Thoroughly whisk together eggs and buttermilk. Pour into a shallow dish and soak sandwiches in a single

layer, about 10 to 20 seconds on each side.

In a large skillet, heat 1 Tbsp butter over medium-high heat. Add 2 sandwiches and cook until golden brown, about 2 minutes per side. Cook remaining sandwiches, adding more butter as needed. Transfer sandwiches onto baking sheet and bake in preheated oven for 5 to 8 minutes, or until cheese has melted.

CARAMELIZED ONION RELISH

2 Tbsp butter
3 onions, diced
3 Tbsp brown sugar
3 Tbsp apple cider vinegar

In a medium saucepan, melt butter over medium-high heat, until foam subsides. Add onions and cook over low to medium heat until very soft, about 10 to 15 minutes. Add sugar and apple cider vinegar and cook gently, stirring frequently until onions are golden brown, another 10 to 15 minutes. This relish keeps in the fridge for 4 to 5 days.

HERBED MUSTARD DIP

¼ cup Dijon mustard
¼ cup grainy mustard
2 Tbsp chopped mixed herbs
  (rosemary, thyme, parsley, etc.)

In a small bowl, combine all ingredients until well blended. Serve as a dip for the sandwiches.

CLASSIC FRENCH ONION SOUP

Soup
¼ cup butter
6 medium Vidalia onions,
  thinly sliced
1 tsp salt
2 bay leaves
1 sprig thyme
1 cup sherry
3 Tbsp brandy
6 cups low-sodium beef stock
salt and pepper

Croutons
four ½-inch-thick slices challah
  (or other egg-based bread), cut
  to fit soup bowls
1 Tbsp olive oil
salt

Cheese topping
4 slices aged cheddar cheese,
  cut ⅛ inch thick

To make the soup, melt butter over medium heat in a heavy-bottomed saucepan. Add onions, salt, bay leaves, and thyme. Cook until onions are softened and start to colour. Reduce heat to medium-low and continue cooking until onions are very soft and deep golden brown, about 45 minutes.

Add sherry and brandy and cook to reduce slightly, about 2 to 3 minutes. Add beef stock and simmer for another 5 to 7 minutes. Season with salt and pepper.

To prepare croutons, preheat oven to 350°F. Brush challah slices lightly with olive oil and season with salt. Toast until golden, about 2 to 3 minutes per side.

To serve, preheat oven broiler. Bring soup to a simmer. Ladle soup into 4 ovenproof bowls, leaving ½ inch at the top. Place croutons on top of soup. Top with cheese. Broil until cheese is melted and bubbling.

7

ALMONDS

Almost two million tons of almonds are produced around the world every year. Although the nut is native to Iran, California produces almost 40 percent of the world's almonds. Almonds are incredibly versatile—they are an integral part of many cultural cuisines, they are the basis of a wide variety of desserts (baklava, nougat, and marzipan), and they are delicious simply roasted and salted. Almonds are high in protein and contain loads of vitamin E, which is great for the skin.

Almonds are also used to manufacture a number of healthy and delicious products. They can be ground into almond butter, which is similar to

GROUND LAMB WITH ROSEMARY AND RAISINS · ALMOND FLATBREAD · ALMOND HUMMUS · PICKLED RED ONIONS

Food is a great way to explore other cultures and push your culinary boundaries right in your own home. Using almonds to make an exotic Middle Eastern main is perfect for shaking up an everyday dinner. I've added them to hummus—a dip made by puréeing or mashing cooked chickpeas with garlic, olive oil, lemon, and tahini (a sesame seed paste)—which has been elemental to Middle Eastern cuisine for thousands of years. There are many versions; this one uses almond oil as well as olive oil, and almond tahini.

Lamb is the Middle East's staple protein, and adding dried fruit to it is an authentic touch. I love how it gives the dish a nice chewy texture. Flatbreads are another fundamental part of Middle Eastern cuisine, and this version is delicious and easy. Once you master it (I promise you'll have it nailed after the first time) you can experiment with the flavours. I love to brush mine with a little garlic butter.

Pickled vegetables are another common item on a Middle Eastern menu. My pickled onions are sweet and tangy with a great crunch, making them the perfect way to cap off this main. {Serves 4}

[TIMING IS EVERYTHING]

Prepare tahini • Prepare hummus and pickled onions • Make flatbread dough • Prepare lamb and keep warm • Bake flatbread • Assemble and serve

GROUND LAMB WITH ROSEMARY AND RAISINS

1 Tbsp olive oil
½ cup diced red onion
2 cloves garlic, finely chopped
1½ lb ground lamb
1 sprig rosemary, leaves only
1 bay leaf
½ cup raisins or chopped dried apricots
1½ cups red wine
salt and pepper

Heat oil in a large saucepan over medium-high heat. Add onion and sauté 2 to 3 minutes. Add garlic and sauté 1 to 2 minutes, or until fragrant.

Add ground lamb, rosemary, and bay leaf. Sauté until excess liquid evaporates and meat is lightly browned. Add raisins and stir to combine. Add red wine to deglaze pan, making sure to scrape up brown bits. Remove from heat and season with salt and pepper. Keep warm until ready to serve.

ALMOND FLATBREAD

1 cup warm water
1 tsp quick-rising yeast
2 cups all-purpose flour
⅓ cup ground almonds
1 tsp whole cumin seeds
1 tsp salt

In a bowl of a stand mixer, stir together water and yeast. Let stand 5 minutes, or until a foam develops. Add flour, ground almonds, cumin, and salt. Mix with the paddle attachment on low speed until dough pulls away from the sides of the bowl (if dough seems sticky, add more flour 1 Tbsp at a time). Switch to dough hook and work 5 minutes on low speed, until dough becomes smooth and elastic. Cover and allow to rise for 20 to 30 minutes in a warm place.

Preheat oven to 425°F.

Divide dough into 8 pieces. Roll into balls and flatten each with hands or a rolling pin.

Place dough onto a baking sheet and bake for 10 minutes. Flip and place directly on oven rack, and bake for another 10 minutes, or until golden brown.

ALMOND HUMMUS

one 14 oz can chickpeas, drained and rinsed
1 cup almond tahini (below)
¼ cup almond oil
¼ cup olive oil
½ clove garlic, minced
juice and zest of 1 lemon
salt

In a food processor or blender, combine chickpeas, almond tahini, almond oil, olive oil, garlic, lemon juice, and zest together until smooth. Transfer to a bowl and season with salt.

Almond tahini

1½ cups ground almonds
⅓ cup almond oil
salt

Lightly toast ground almonds in a dry skillet until golden brown. In a food processor or blender, combine ground almonds and almond oil until smooth. Season with salt.

PICKLED RED ONIONS

1 cup water
½ cup red wine vinegar
¼ cup sugar
1 bay leaf
pinch of salt
½ red onion, sliced

In a medium saucepan, bring water, red wine vinegar, sugar, bay leaf, and salt to a boil. Add red onion, remove from heat, and let cool, covered, for 15 minutes. Drain and serve.

TO SERVE

½ cup sliced almonds, toasted
1 Tbsp chopped cilantro
½ tsp paprika (smoked or sweet)

Spread hummus on a large plate. Top with lamb, toasted almonds, pickled onions, cilantro, and paprika. Serve with flatbread.

AVOCADO

Rich in taste and buttery in texture, avocados have always been treasured—they were once considered a luxury food and reserved for royals. Often mistaken for a vegetable, avocado is a sumptuous fruit originating from south central Mexico, where it has been cultivated for thousands of years.

With their oval shape and textured green skin that turns deep purple as it ripens, avocados have earned the nickname "alligator pear." There are many varieties of avocado, including Fuerte, Gwen, Hass, Lamb Hass, Pinkerton, Reed, and Zutano. Hass is the most common and is also known as the "year-round avocado" because of

BEEF AND AVOCADO LETTUCE WRAPS WITH TOMATO, BACON, AND BLUE CHEESE · POTATO AND AVOCADO SALAD WITH HEARTS OF PALM

This main combines super-healthy foods in a colourful meal that tastes incredible. The lettuce wraps are loaded with ingredients that complement each other nicely; the bacon's smoky flavour and crunchy texture provides a contrast to the tenderness of the filet mignon. The tomatoes balance the meats with a fresh, juicy acidity and a burst of colour. The grilled guacamole unites the buttery

softness of avocado with the bite of hot sauce and the tang of lime juice. Wrapping all this great food up in tender Boston lettuce (also known as bibb or butter lettuce) is a fun, healthy, and delicious way to eat—it's all flavour! The simple and unique avocado and potato side salad rounds out this main by putting the lovely flavour of the avocado front and centre. {Serves 4}

BEEF AND AVOCADO LETTUCE WRAPS WITH TOMATO, BACON, AND BLUE CHEESE

Dressing

¼ cup red wine vinegar
2 Tbsp finely chopped shallots
  (or red onion)
1 Tbsp finely chopped jalapeño
¾ cup olive oil
salt and pepper

Grilled guacamole

2 avocados, cut in half, pitted,
  and peeled
4 Tbsp avocado oil (divided)
juice of 1 lime
¼ tsp hot sauce, or to taste
pinch of sugar
salt and pepper

Wraps

1 bunch green onions, cut in half
  and ends trimmed
1 Tbsp olive oil
salt and pepper
4 Tbsp prepared dressing (divided)
8 strips bacon
two 4 oz centre-cut beef tenderloins
  (filet mignon)
4 hard-boiled eggs, coarsely
  chopped
2 tomatoes, diced
2 heads Boston lettuce, cleaned and
  leaves removed
½ cup crumbled blue cheese

For the dressing, combine red wine vinegar, shallots, and jalapeño in a medium bowl. Add olive oil in a slow stream, whisking to combine. Season with salt and pepper. Set aside.

For the grilled guacamole, preheat barbecue or indoor grill to medium-high heat. Brush avocado with 1 Tbsp avocado oil. Grill avocado 1 to 2 minutes per side, or until lightly charred. Let cool and cut into chunks. Mash avocado chunks with a fork in a small bowl. Add remaining 3 Tbsp avocado oil, lime juice, hot sauce, and sugar. Season with salt and pepper. Set aside.

Preheat oven to 375°F.

Place green onions on a sheet of aluminum foil, drizzle with olive oil, and season with salt and pepper. Wrap package into a bundle and bake in preheated oven for 15 to 20 minutes, or until tender. Remove from oven and let cool. Coarsely chop onions. Toss with 2 Tbsp of dressing, and set aside in a serving bowl.

Place bacon on a rack set over a baking sheet. Bake in preheated oven 15 minutes, or until crisp and golden. Transfer to a paper towel–lined plate to cool, then cut into ½-inch pieces. Set aside.

Season beef tenderloin steaks with salt and pepper. In a large cast iron skillet, over medium-high heat, sear meat 2 to 3 minutes per side, or until medium-rare. Remove from heat and allow to rest 3 to 4 minutes. Cut meat into bite-sized pieces. Toss with 2 Tbsp of dressing, and set aside in a serving bowl. Set remaining dressing aside for the potato and avocado salad. Place eggs, tomatoes, and blue cheese in small serving bowls.

Let your guests assemble their own wraps by taking 1 lettuce leaf and filling it with green onions, bacon, beef, eggs, tomatoes, grilled guacamole, and blue cheese. You should get approximately 12 wraps.

POTATO AND AVOCADO SALAD WITH HEARTS OF PALM

½ lb mini white potatoes
one 14 oz can hearts of palm,
  cut into ½-inch pieces
2 avocados, peeled and cut into
  large chunks
½ cup prepared dressing (see left)

Boil potatoes until tender, about 8 to 10 minutes. Let cool. Slice potatoes in half. In a large bowl, combine potatoes, hearts of palm, and avocado. Add dressing and toss to combine.

BASIL

Basil originated in India, where it has been cultivated for over five thousand years. There are many varieties of the herb, ranging in flavours from lemon to mint and in colours from green to purple. Italian basil is the Mediterranean's most popular herb. It has broad tender leaves, a pungent floral aroma, and a mild anise flavour. Basil translates to "king" in Greek and is commonly regarded as the "king of herbs" because of its versatility in both sweet and savoury dishes.

Pesto is one of the most common culinary uses of basil. Pesto is almost as versatile as basil itself—it can be used as a sauce, dip, dressing,

garnish, seasoning, or spread. There are many
variations on pesto, but the most popular
originates from Genoa, Italy. To make Genovese
pesto, grind basil, garlic, and pine nuts together
in a pesto mortar. Once these ingredients are
mixed, add olive oil for a smooth consistency and
fruity flavour.

BROILED TILAPIA WITH CHERRY TOMATO CONFIT · SAUTÉED CHORIZO, OLIVES, AND ARTICHOKES · ORZO WITH FRESH PESTO

This is a truly Mediterranean main—it features staple ingredients from throughout the region and showcases them in their purest forms. This meal also highlights basil's versatility: pesto enhances the mild tilapia, while basil brings a fresh aroma to the Sautéed Chorizo, Olives, and Artichokes and infuses the tomato confit with flavour. If you can't find tilapia, use snapper, striped bass, halibut, or haddock instead.

Confit is a French culinary term that refers to slowly cooking an ingredient in its own juices or fat. Confit of duck is a common example. Duck legs are submerged in duck fat and cooked slowly until they're tender. Like many culinary terms, however, the principle is open to interpretation. I like to "confit" vegetables in olive oil. The key is to get the oil just hot enough. If it's too hot, the tomatoes will essentially deep-fry and fall apart. Oil is an incredible conductor of flavours, so this is a great opportunity to infuse it with basil and garlic, which will then cook right into the cherry tomatoes. Yum! This Mediterranean main is absolutely delicious as one cohesive meal, or the dishes can also be enjoyed separately as appetizers, antipasto, or tapas. *{Serves 4}*

BROILED TILAPIA WITH CHERRY TOMATO CONFIT

Tilapia
four 5 oz tilapia fillets, skin removed
1 Tbsp olive oil
4 Tbsp fresh pesto (see right)
salt and pepper
1 lemon, halved

Cherry tomato confit
½ cup olive oil
1 clove garlic, crushed
1 basil sprig
½ pint whole cherry tomatoes
salt

Preheat oven broiler to high.

For the tilapia, place fillets in a roasting pan. Drizzle with olive oil and rub to coat the fish. Spread each fillet with 1 Tbsp of pesto. Season fish with salt and pepper. Broil 4 to 5 minutes, or until cooked through. Remove from oven and squeeze lemon juice over pan to loosen fish. Combine lemon juice with residual olive oil and pan juices.

For the confit, in a medium saucepan, heat oil, garlic, and basil over medium heat. Add tomatoes. Poach for 10 minutes, or until tomatoes break out of their skin.

Remove from heat and season with salt.

SAUTÉED CHORIZO, OLIVES, AND ARTICHOKES

1 tsp olive oil
1 chorizo sausage, sliced into coins
4 canned artichoke hearts, packed in water or oil, halved
¼ cup whole black olives, pitted
8–10 capers
3 basil leaves, torn

In a medium skillet, heat olive oil. Add chorizo and sauté 3 to 4 minutes, or until crispy.

Add artichoke hearts and sauté another 2 to 3 minutes, or until golden. Add olives and capers and cook over medium heat until mixture comes together, about 1 to 2 minutes. Remove from heat and stir in torn basil.

ORZO WITH FRESH PESTO

Pasta
1½ cups orzo pasta

Fresh pesto
3 large garlic cloves
3 cups loosely packed fresh basil
½ cup pine nuts
⅔ cup coarsely grated Parmigiano-Reggiano (about 2 oz)
1 tsp salt
½ tsp black pepper
⅔ cup extra virgin olive oil

Cook orzo in a large pot of salted water according to package directions. Rinse and drain well.

In a food processor or blender, finely chop garlic cloves. Add basil, pine nuts, Parmigiano-Reggiano, and salt and pepper, and process until finely chopped.

With motor running, add oil, blending until incorporated. If pesto seems dry, add more olive oil, 1 Tbsp at a time. Set 4 Tbsp of pesto aside for Tilapia and toss remaining pesto with prepared orzo.

19

BUTTERNUT SQUASH

Butternut squash is a "hard squash" (as opposed to zucchini, for example, which is a soft variety). It has a smooth beige shell and vibrant yellow-to-orange flesh, and usually weighs between two and three pounds. Cooked butternut squash has a sweet nutty taste and buttery texture. Compared

and very easy to work with. Although its season peaks in late summer, butternut can be enjoyed all year round. This golden beauty is high in vitamins C and E and fibre and is tasty prepared in a variety of ways; serve it baked, roasted, mashed, crushed, or puréed.

When shopping for butternut squash, look for a uniformly coloured shell free of cracks and spots. Avoid squash with shiny or green-tinged shells, sure signs that they've been picked early and aren't as sweet as they could be. Generally speaking, larger squash are more developed and sweeter. Butternut squash is good for the long haul—it'll last for up to six weeks in a cool dry place or about a week in the fridge.

ROSEMARY AND HONEY GLAZED CHICKEN · CRUSHED BUTTERNUT SQUASH WITH FRIED SAGE · CRISPY SHALLOTS · BUTTERED SPINACH

Butternut squash is one of my favourite squash, and it's this recipe that really made me crazy about the stuff. The brown butter gives the squash a wonderfully nutty and warm appeal, which pairs beautifully with the chicken's elegant white wine, honey, and rosemary glaze. If you can, always go for free-range and organic poultry. While there is a price attached, it tends to be more moist and flavourful than its mass-produced counterpart and has a nice yellow-coloured fat. This recipe calls for chicken breast supreme, which is simply a chicken breast, skin on, with the wing bone still attached. You can also use plain chicken breasts.

Fried shallots—a staple in Scandinavian cooking—top the dish off beautifully by adding an onion flavour and a lovely crunchy texture. I was introduced to fried shallots by my dad's girlfriend, who puts them on her mashed potatoes. She's quite the cook! {Serves 4}

ROSEMARY AND HONEY GLAZED CHICKEN

½ cup white wine
¼ cup honey
2 sprigs rosemary
½ tsp black pepper
4 chicken breasts supreme
salt and pepper
1 Tbsp butter

Preheat oven to 350°F.

In a small saucepan set over medium heat, simmer white wine and honey until liquid has reduced by a third. Add rosemary and pepper. Remove glaze from heat and set aside for basting.

Season chicken with salt and pepper. In a large ovenproof sauté pan set over medium-high heat, sear chicken breasts, skin side down, for 5 to 6 minutes, or until fat has rendered and skin is golden and crispy. Remove from heat and let cool for 2 minutes. Flip chicken. Add butter to pan with chicken and place in preheated oven. Cook for 8 to 10 minutes, or until chicken is cooked through, basting with prepared glaze periodically.

CRUSHED BUTTERNUT SQUASH WITH FRIED SAGE

1 Tbsp olive oil
2 medium butternut squash, peeled and cut into large chunks
3 Tbsp butter (divided)

6–8 sage leaves, coarsely chopped
1 clove garlic, crushed
juice of ½ lemon
salt and pepper

Preheat oven to 350°F.

In a medium ovenproof skillet, heat olive oil. Add butternut squash and cook 3 to 4 minutes, or until lightly coloured. Add 2 Tbsp of butter and cook another 3 to 4 minutes to allow squash to brown slightly.

Place pan in preheated oven and roast squash for 25 to 30 minutes, or until tender. Remove from oven and transfer squash to a bowl.

Add remaining 1 Tbsp butter, sage, garlic, and lemon juice to hot skillet and cook over medium heat for 1 to 2 minutes, or until butter is foaming and sage is crackling. Add butter mixture to squash and crush squash to allow flavours to come together.

CRISPY SHALLOTS

3 cups vegetable oil for frying
3 large shallots, peeled and thinly sliced
1 Tbsp cornstarch
salt

In a large saucepan, heat oil to 350°F.

In a medium bowl, toss shallot rings with cornstarch. Add shallots to oil and cook until lightly browned, 2 to 3 minutes (they will continue to brown once removed from oil). While frying, be sure to move them around with a strainer or spider. Transfer to a paper towel–lined plate and sprinkle with salt. Keep warm.

BUTTERED SPINACH

1 Tbsp butter
8 oz bag fresh spinach, washed

In a large skillet, melt butter over medium heat. Add spinach and sauté until slightly wilted, 3 to 4 minutes. Serve with shallot rings and pan drippings from chicken.

23

CAPERS

Capers are the bud (or berries) of the caper shrub, a perennial plant that grows throughout the Mediterranean. Capers are picked prematurely, when they are still olive green in colour, and then cured in a briny mixture of salt and vinegar. If the buds are allowed to mature, they become

approximately three to four times the size of what we commonly call "capers" and are known as "caper buds." Traditionally a staple ingredient throughout Mediterranean regions, capers have become hugely popular in North American and European kitchens. They can be used in many

MY GRANDMOTHER'S PORK
ROULADEN · CAULIFLOWER CHEESE GRATIN
WITH CAPERS · PICKLED CUCUMBER
SALAD WITH FRESH DILL

My oma (grandmother) used to make an award-winning (in my books!) cauliflower soup, which was my first taste of the vegetable. In this gratin, tender cauliflower bubbles away in a creamy cheese sauce with rosemary, garlic, and golden breadcrumbs. Capers bring a lovely saltiness to the dish that really makes it pop.

Pork Rouladen is another one of my oma's signature dishes and one of the top ten most delicious things I've ever eaten: paper-thin slices of pork brushed with spicy Dijon mustard, stuffed with pickles and capers, wrapped in bacon, and seared to perfection. What's not to love?

This is a real meal. It's hearty and on the richer side. A simple, crisp, and refreshing pickled cucumber salad on the side keeps it balanced. *{Serves 4}*

MY GRANDMOTHER'S PORK ROULADEN

4 pork cutlets (centre-cut pork tenderloin)

salt and pepper

2 tsp Dijon mustard

2 tsp thyme leaves

8 pickles

3 Tbsp chopped capers

8 slices bacon

2 Tbsp vegetable oil

¾ cup white wine (divided)

5–6 sprigs thyme

3 Tbsp sour cream

1 Tbsp grainy mustard

Preheat oven to 350°F.

In between two pieces of plastic wrap, pound each piece of pork to ¼-inch thickness. Cut each piece in half. Season each piece of pork with salt and pepper. Spread ½ tsp of Dijon mustard on each and sprinkle with thyme leaves. Place pickles on short end of pork (1 pickle on each piece), and sprinkle entire surface with capers. Starting at the short end, roll pork into a cigar shape (away from you) and wrap each bundle with a slice of bacon. Tie each pork bundle with butcher's twine. Repeat with remaining pieces of pork.

In a large skillet, heat oil over medium-high heat. Sear pork rolls on all sides, about 5 to 6 minutes, or until bacon is crispy.

Add ½ cup white wine to deglaze, making sure to scrape up all the brown bits. Add thyme sprigs.

Transfer skillet to preheated oven and continue cooking pork another 4 to 5 minutes, or until cooked through.

Remove from oven and transfer pork rolls to another dish. Add remaining ¼ cup white wine, sour cream, and grainy mustard to skillet. Stir to combine. Slice Rouladen and serve with pan sauce.

CAULIFLOWER CHEESE GRATIN WITH CAPERS

2 medium white potatoes, peeled and cut into quarters

1 medium head of cauliflower, broken into florets

2 cups whipping cream (35%)

2 Tbsp butter

1 clove garlic, minced

2 sprigs rosemary

1 bay leaf

pinch of nutmeg

salt and pepper

¼ cup breadcrumbs

1 cup grated Emmenthal, Swiss, or Gouda cheese

2 Tbsp capers

chopped fresh rosemary, for garnish

Preheat oven to 400°F.

Place potatoes in a small saucepan and cover with cold water. Bring to a simmer and cook 12 to 15 minutes, or until potatoes are fork tender. Drain potatoes and put through a ricer. Set aside.

Meanwhile, cook cauliflower in a large pot of salted water for 5 to 8 minutes, or until tender. Drain and set aside.

In a large saucepan, bring whipping cream to a simmer. Add butter, garlic, rosemary, bay leaf, nutmeg, and salt and pepper to taste. Add cooked potatoes and cauliflower and stir to combine.

Transfer mixture to an 8- x 10-inch ovenproof casserole dish. Sprinkle with half of the breadcrumbs and then the cheese. Top with remaining breadcrumbs and capers.

Bake in preheated oven for 40 to 45 minutes, or until bubbling and golden brown on top. Sprinkle with chopped rosemary before serving.

PICKLED CUCUMBER SALAD WITH FRESH DILL

1 English cucumber, thinly sliced

2 Tbsp white wine vinegar

1 Tbsp sugar

1 tsp salt

¼ cup chopped dill

In a medium bowl, combine cucumbers, white wine vinegar, sugar, and salt. Add chopped dill and toss to coat.

27

CHICKEN WINGS

There's no doubt that the first restaurant to serve Buffalo wings was in Buffalo, New York, hence the name. Which Buffalo restaurant it was, however, is very much open to dispute. Regardless of where they were first served, the popularity of chicken wings spread like wildfire and they are now a staple in restaurants, bars, and pubs worldwide. In fact, July 29th is officially dubbed "Chicken Wing Day" in Buffalo.

Classic chicken wings feature a deep-fried wing and/or drumette doused in a combination of hot sauce and butter. They are traditionally served

ASIAN-STYLE BAKED CHICKEN WINGS · **BLUE CHEESE AND BUTTERMILK DRESSING** · CRISPY FRIED CELERIAC WEDGES · **CARROT-CELERY SLAW WITH TOASTED GARLIC AND LEMON DRESSING**

With its Asian spin, this main ups the ante on a classic hot wing. I haven't removed any of the key components of a great plate of wings, but rather added my own spin and style. I like to bake my wings because it gives me the opportunity to marinate them in straight-up flavour first, and I love the way a marinade bakes right into the chicken as it cooks. You can't marinate a wing that you intend to fry, because the marinade will

When it comes to wings, the refreshing crunch of celery is an exquisite accompaniment. I've thrown it down with julienned carrots in a sweet, crunchy slaw. Blue cheese is another essential part of the wing experience. My simple dressing balances the saltiness of the cheese with the tang of buttermilk and the acidity of red wine vinegar. *{Serves 4}*

[TIMING IS EVERYTHING]
*Assemble marinade and add chicken wings; refrigerate • Make blue cheese
dressing and slaw (can be made up to 3 hours in advance and refrigerated) •
Bake wings and prepare wedges • Fry wedges and keep warm • Remove wings
from oven and serve*

ASIAN-STYLE BAKED CHICKEN WINGS

¾ cup ketjap manis (Indonesian
   soy sauce)
¼ cup oyster sauce
¼ cup chopped cilantro stems
1 bunch green onions, coarsely
   chopped
4 cloves garlic, peeled and finely
   chopped
2 Tbsp Sriracha sauce (Thai hot
   sauce)
2 Tbsp sesame oil
1½-inch piece fresh ginger, peeled
   and coarsely chopped
20 chicken wings
2 Tbsp sesame seeds, toasted

In a large bowl, combine ketjap
manis, oyster sauce, cilantro stems,
green onions, garlic, Sriracha sauce,
sesame oil, and chopped ginger. Add
chicken wings and marinate for at

least 20 minutes, and up to overnight,
in the refrigerator.

Preheat oven to 450°F.

Transfer chicken wings to a large
ovenproof dish. Pour marinade over
wings. Place in preheated oven and
bake for 20 minutes. Reduce oven
temperature to 350°F and bake
another 40 to 45 minutes. Sprinkle
with sesame seeds. Serve hot.

BLUE CHEESE AND BUTTERMILK DRESSING

1½ cups crumbled blue cheese
½ cup buttermilk
1 tsp red wine vinegar
freshly ground black pepper

In a blender, combine blue cheese,
buttermilk, and red wine vinegar.
Blend until smooth. Season with black
pepper. Keep refrigerated until ready
to serve.

CRISPY FRIED CELERIAC WEDGES

1 head celeriac (celery root), peeled
   and cut into wedges
2 cups all-purpose flour
4 eggs
2 cups panko (Japanese
   breadcrumbs)
½ cup chopped parsley
1 tsp freshly ground black pepper
1½ tsp salt
zest of 1 lemon
vegetable oil for frying
celery salt, for sprinkling

Fill a large pot with cold salted water.
Add celeriac and bring to a boil.
Reduce to a simmer and cook for 15 to
20 minutes, or until celeriac is tender.
Drain in a colander.

Place flour in a shallow dish and set
aside. Whisk eggs in another shallow
dish and set aside. In a third dish, mix
panko, parsley, black pepper, salt, and
lemon zest.

Working in batches, toss celeriac in
flour, shaking off excess. Place in eggs
to coat and then in panko mixture.
Lay on a baking sheet.

In a large heavy pot, add enough
oil to reach 4 inches in depth. Heat
oil to 360°F. Fry breaded celeriac
for 4 to 6 minutes, or until golden.
Remove from oil and drain on a paper
towel–lined plate. Sprinkle with
celery salt.

CARROT-CELERY SLAW WITH TOASTED GARLIC AND LEMON DRESSING

4 celery stalks, julienned
1 large carrot, julienned
3 Tbsp vegetable oil
2 cloves garlic, peeled and finely
   chopped
juice of 1 lemon
salt and pepper

In a medium bowl, mix together
julienned celery and carrot.

In a small skillet, heat vegetable
oil over medium heat. Add garlic
and sauté for 2 to 3 minutes, or until
golden brown. Remove from heat
and pour oil over celery and carrot.
Add lemon juice and toss to combine.
Season with salt and pepper. Keep
refrigerated until ready to serve.

CHILIES

A product of the capsicum plant, the chili pepper has been a staple ingredient in Mexican cuisine for centuries. It was introduced to Asia by European explorers and soon became an integral element of many regional cuisines—Korean, Indian, Indonesian, Szechuan, Vietnamese, and Thai.

There are many different varieties of chilies. Red and green are the most common; they range in heat from sweet and mild to fiery hot.

The heat in chilies comes from a chemical compound that the human body registers as an irritant. This chemical prompts the body to produce

endorphins, which act as a natural painkiller and can cause feelings of euphoria. If you don't like eating super-spicy foods, you can reduce a chili's heat by discarding the membrane and seeds (where the active chemical is found) and

Chilies can be used fresh, dried, or ground into a powder. They're also used in many dips and sauces, from hot sauce to sweet chili sauce, and from Sriracha to sambal. The leaves can be sautéed and served as greens.

CHILI SHRIMP·MANGO NOODLE SALAD·VIETNAMESE SPRING ROLLS·SWEET CHILI DIPPING SAUCE

I really love Thai, Szechuan, Cambodian, and Vietnamese cuisines. The combination of fresh vegetables, exotic fruits, kaleidoscopic colours, and firecracker flavours makes for a truly exciting culinary experience. The Chili Shrimp combines the delicate shellfish with the spice of serrano chili, the nutty aroma of sesame oil, the tang of lime, and the unique bite of fresh ginger.

My travels through Thailand, where mangoes are abundant, inspire the salad. I've featured the fruit alongside chayote and cucumber for their refreshing crunch, red and green onion for a savoury bite, and fresh cilantro for its floral aroma. Crushed cashews are the ultimate crunchy way to top it all off.

The Vietnamese make the best spring rolls—and dipping sauce, for that matter! They traditionally use rice paper instead of egg-roll wrappers, making the spring rolls super-crunchy, sticky, and chewy when they're fried, which sets these rolls apart. {Serves 4}

CHILI SHRIMP

1 Tbsp vegetable oil

2 cloves garlic, sliced

1 shallot, sliced

12 medium-sized shrimp, peeled, deveined, tails removed, and sliced in half lengthwise

1 green serrano chili, sliced

1 red serrano chili, sliced

1 tsp sesame oil

juice of ½ lime

½ tsp freshly grated ginger

salt

In a medium sauté pan, heat vegetable oil over medium heat. Add garlic and shallot and cook 2 to 3 minutes, or until lightly coloured. Add shrimp and chilies and cook 1 to 2 minutes, tossing occasionally. Add sesame oil, lime juice, and ginger. Stir to combine. Remove from heat and season with salt. Set aside.

MANGO NOODLE SALAD

1 package cellophane noodles (½ lb)

4 green onions, thinly sliced

2 firm and not fully ripe mangoes, peeled and julienned

1 chayote, julienned

½ cucumber, julienned

½ red onion, thinly sliced, soaked in cold water for 10 minutes, and drained

½ cup cilantro leaves

½ cup Sweet Chili Dipping Sauce

⅓ cup cashews, toasted and crushed

Soak cellophane noodles in warm water for about 20 minutes. Drain well and, using a pair of scissors, snip noodles into shorter lengths.

In a large bowl, toss green onions, mangoes, chayote, cucumber, red onion, and cilantro. Add ½ cup Sweet Chili Dipping Sauce to coat.

Place salad mixture over a bed of cellophane noodles. Top with reserved Chili Shrimp and cashews.

VIETNAMESE SPRING ROLLS

2 Tbsp vegetable oil

3 cups sliced shiitake mushrooms, stems removed

1 clove garlic, finely chopped

3 green onions, finely chopped

1 Tbsp chopped ginger

10 oz minced pork

2 tsp balsamic vinegar

1 tsp sesame oil

1 tsp fish sauce

1 tsp sugar

1 tsp cornstarch

salt and white pepper

10–12 rice paper wrappers

vegetable oil for frying

In a medium skillet, heat 2 Tbsp vegetable oil over medium-high heat. Add mushrooms and sauté 3 to 4 minutes, or until soft. Add garlic and sauté another 2 to 3 minutes, or until garlic is fragrant. Remove from heat and stir in green onions and ginger. Allow mixture to cool.

Add minced pork, balsamic vinegar, sesame oil, fish sauce, sugar, cornstarch, and salt and white pepper. Combine well with hands and form pork mixture into a ball. Holding pork mixture in one hand and bowl in the other, throw pork into bowl from a distance of 10 to 15 inches, repeating about 10 times. This allows the meat to bind together.

Work in batches by soaking about 5 rice paper wrappers at a time in warm water. Remove from water and lay on a work surface to allow papers to dry out slightly.

Place 3 Tbsp of pork mixture in a 3-inch-long strip across the bottom of a wrapper (about 1 inch from the bottom). Fold bottom of wrapper over filling, then fold in sides. Roll up tightly, pressing to seal edge. Repeat with remaining wrappers and pork mixture.

In a large heavy pot, pour oil to a depth of about 4 inches. Heat to 350°F. Working in batches, fry rolls in oil for about 5 to 8 minutes, or until crispy and light golden brown. Drain on a paper towel–lined plate. Repeat with remaining spring rolls. Keep warm until ready to serve. Serve with Sweet Chili Dipping Sauce.

SWEET CHILI DIPPING SAUCE

½ cup fish sauce

½ cup water

½ cup sugar

2 Tbsp rice vinegar

juice of 2 limes

2 red chilies, finely chopped

2 green chilies, finely chopped

In a small bowl, combine fish sauce, water, sugar, rice vinegar, lime juice, and red and green chilies.

CIDER VINEGAR

Cider is a drink made by pressing the juice from apples (and sometimes pears). Before the juice is allowed to ferment and become alcoholic, it's referred to as "sweet cider." After fermentation, when alcohol is present, it is known as "hard cider." If this fermentation process is taken even further, it becomes apple cider vinegar.

Vinegar, which is often associated with grapes and wine-making, is derived from the Latin *vinum acer*, which translates to "sour wine." Vinegar is key in my cooking; I love using good-quality vinegar to finish rich meat sauces, in a *jus*, or in braised dishes like ribs. I like to keep a few top-shelf vinegars in my pantry. It's a worthy

investment—they last for years, and just a few drops can put a sauce, salad, or an entire main right over the top. There are a lot of fine vinegars out there; world-class balsamic and sherry vinegars are often highly regarded, in the same way as award-winning wines. This doesn't mean you have to drop your entire paycheque to play, though. Check out your local French, Italian, or Spanish market and you're sure to find some real treasures without breaking the bank.

SLOW-COOKED TANGY SHORT RIBS • **COLESLAW WITH APPLE CIDER VINAIGRETTE** • TWICE-BAKED POTATOES WITH THE GOODS

I consider myself a bit of a connoisseur when it comes to ribs, and this recipe sets the bar high. The succulent, rich flavour of short ribs is perfectly balanced by the sweet, crisp acidity of apple cider vinegar. The *gastrique* (a combination of sugar and vinegar) gives the dish a delicious sweet and sour flavour. Coleslaw and potatoes are classic sides for ribs, and these versions are amazing. Salting and draining the cabbage for the coleslaw removes all its bitterness and makes it nice and tender. The tart apple cider vinegar dressing is a nice departure from the creamy stuff we're all used to. The twice-baked potatoes are another creative twist on a classic dish and a nice companion to the ribs.

I positively love sweet and tangy, finger-licking short ribs—a quintessential summer food. Some of my favourite recipes showcase humble, relatively inexpensive cuts like short ribs. It's the cooking technique and time you invest into preparing a cut like this that gives you that moist, fall-off-the-bone effect. This recipe may be simple, but a word of advice: make extra! {Serves 4}

[TIMING IS EVERYTHING]

Prepare coleslaw and refrigerate • Bake potatoes and cool • Sear ribs, make sauce, and braise in oven • Make potato filling and re-stuff • Remove ribs from oven and reduce sauce • Heat stuffed potatoes

SLOW-COOKED TANGY SHORT RIBS

four 12 oz portions short ribs, each
  cut into 3-inch lengths
salt and pepper
3 Tbsp vegetable oil
1 medium onion, roughly chopped
2 bay leaves
3 cloves garlic, crushed
4 whole cloves
2 sprigs rosemary
2 sprigs thyme
2 Tbsp tomato paste
¾ cup apple cider vinegar
¾ cup brown sugar
¼ cup white wine
4 cups beef stock
2 Tbsp black pepper

Preheat oven to 325°F.

Season ribs with salt and pepper. Heat vegetable oil in a large, wide, ovenproof skillet with high sides (a Dutch oven is perfect) over high heat. Add ribs and sear on all sides until deep golden brown. Transfer seared ribs to a plate or tray.

In same skillet, sweat onion, bay leaves, garlic, cloves, rosemary, and thyme until lightly coloured, about 5 minutes. Add tomato paste and *cook out* for 2 minutes (see page 86). Deglaze pan with apple cider vinegar; add brown sugar and bring to a simmer. Add white wine, beef stock, and pepper; bring to a simmer. Skim off fat from the surface. Return ribs to skillet and place in preheated oven, loosely covered. Braise until ribs are tender, about 60 minutes.

Remove ribs from braising liquid and set aside. Discard rosemary and thyme stems. Remove all but 3 cups of braising liquid; return skillet to stove and reduce volume by two-thirds, over medium heat, skimming if necessary. Sauce should be glaze consistency. Adjust seasoning with salt and pepper; pour glaze over ribs and lightly toss to coat.

COLESLAW WITH APPLE CIDER VINAIGRETTE

½ medium cabbage, thinly sliced
  (about 5 cups)
2 Tbsp salt
¼ cup apple cider vinegar
3 Tbsp sugar
¼ cup vegetable oil
1 Tbsp dried mustard
1 tsp caraway seeds
salt and pepper
1 small carrot, grated

Combine cabbage with salt; place in a large colander for about 60 minutes to drain. Rinse and pat dry.

Combine apple cider vinegar, sugar, oil, mustard, and caraway seeds in a medium pot. Stir over medium heat just until sugar dissolves. Remove from heat. Season with salt and pepper. Cool completely.

Combine cabbage with grated carrot in a large bowl; add dressing and toss to coat. Cover and refrigerate for at least 60 minutes.

TWICE-BAKED POTATOES WITH THE GOODS

4 medium baking potatoes
2 Tbsp butter
2 Tbsp chopped chives or
  green onion
1 cup grated cheese (mozzarella,
  Edam, or Monterey Jack)
salt and pepper
¼ cup sour cream
extra chopped chives for garnish
  (optional)

Preheat oven to 400°F.

Wrap potatoes in aluminum foil; arrange on a tray and bake until centres are tender, about 45 minutes. When cool enough to handle, split potatoes in half; scoop out insides and place them in a medium bowl, reserving skins. Roughly mash potato. Add butter, chives, and ½ cup of the cheese. Season with salt and pepper.

Carefully stuff filling back into potato skins and top with remaining cheese. Arrange on tray and bake again until cheese is melted, about 5 minutes. Garnish with sour cream and chopped chives, if desired.

CLAMS

The sweet and salty flavour of clams makes them the perfect addition to a variety of dishes. Larger cherrystone clams are ideal for roasting because they're meaty and can stand the heat of the oven. Littleneck clams are a smaller, more delicate variety; they are incredibly tender and perfect for pastas. It's always important to take into

account the simple sweetness of clams when combining them with other ingredients. Clams, along with many other shellfish, can be over-powered by too many flavours, and are best prepared and served simply.

When you're buying clams, always look for the freshest live clams you can find. Fresh clams

LINGUINE WITH CLAMS, GARLIC, AND WHITE WINE · FRIED BREADCRUMBS · BAKED CLAMS WITH CHORIZO AND FINGERLING POTATOES

Clams are so straightforward to work with that it's simple enough to prepare these two killer mains without breaking a sweat.

The pasta dish pairs the clam's natural sweetness with meaty pancetta. In Italian cuisine, a very small amount of cured meat is often used to flavour an entire dish, and that's exactly the case with this little number: simple flavour combinations and a dead-easy preparation result in one truly remarkable dish. This one is great for impressing a first date and is easy enough for the busiest of weeknights.

The baked clam dish might have traditionally been cooked over an open fire on a beach in Spain, and it's important to mimic that high heat and roasting effect in your oven at home. This is the ultimate in rustic cuisine, with just a handful of simple and delicious ingredients front and centre. Try dipping crusty bread in the broth at the bottom of the pan. If there's any leftover liquid, strain and freeze it. It's a great addition to a seafood bisque or chowder. {Serves 4}

LINGUINE WITH CLAMS, GARLIC, AND WHITE WINE

3 Tbsp olive oil
2 Tbsp diced pancetta
  (about 2 slices)
2 cloves garlic, thinly sliced
2 shallots, thinly sliced
pinch of chili flakes
2 lb clams, cleaned and scrubbed
½ cup white wine
½ cup canned baby clams (reserve
  2 Tbsp clam juice)
2 Tbsp butter
salt and pepper
1 lb dried linguine
¼ cup chopped flat leaf parsley
Fried Breadcrumbs

Heat olive oil in a large heavy-bottomed saucepan over medium heat. Add pancetta and sauté until golden. Stir in garlic, shallots, and chili flakes; sauté until soft and starting to colour. Tumble in fresh clams, then add white wine and reserved clam juice. Turn heat up to medium-high and cover pot tightly with a lid. Cook, shaking pot occasionally, until clams open, about 5 to 6 minutes. Uncover and turn heat down to low. Add baby clams; stir just to warm through. Swirl in butter and season with salt and pepper.

Meanwhile, bring a large pot of salted water to a rolling boil. Cook pasta until al dente, about 8 minutes, or according to package instructions. Drain pasta, reserving ½ cup of pasta cooking water. Toss pasta into clams, coating noodles well. If necessary, add a few tablespoons of cooking water to loosen sauce. Take pot off heat; fold in parsley and drizzle with olive oil.

To serve, divide noodles between serving plates, arranging clams on top. Top with Fried Breadcrumbs, olive oil, and cracked black pepper, if desired.

FRIED BREADCRUMBS

2 Tbsp olive oil
1 clove garlic, finely minced
½ cup crushed breadcrumbs
salt and pepper

Preheat oven to 300°F.

Heat olive oil and garlic in a medium ovenproof skillet over medium heat. Fry garlic for 1 minute, then add breadcrumbs and salt and pepper. Toss to coat breadcrumbs. Place pan in oven and toast until breadcrumbs are golden brown, about 3 to 4 minutes.

BAKED CLAMS WITH CHORIZO AND FINGERLING POTATOES

3 Tbsp olive oil
18–20 small fingerling potatoes
salt and pepper
½ onion, roughly chopped
1 chorizo sausage, cut into ¼-inch-
  thick coins
4 lb cherrystone clams, cleaned and
  scrubbed
½ cup white wine
½ cup chicken stock
1 clove garlic, sliced
1 tsp sweet smoked paprika
¼ cup chopped flat leaf parsley

Preheat oven to 450°F.

Put olive oil and potatoes in a large, wide, ovenproof dish; toss to coat and season with salt and pepper. Roast in oven, about 7 to 10 minutes. Add onion and sausage and return to oven for another 7 to 10 minutes, until onion is coloured and sausage is crispy in places. Add clams, white wine, chicken stock, and garlic to pan and return to oven, roasting for another 13 to 15 minutes, until clams are open and pan juices are bubbling. Sprinkle with paprika and parsley.

43

C O D

Salted cod is a staple of Mediterranean cooking, a legacy from the days before modern methods of preservation like canning and refrigeration. Nowadays, however, fresh cod is available at just about every grocer and fishmonger, and usually for quite a reasonable price. Cod is a simple, firm, and meaty fish with a relatively mild flavour. I particularly love cod because it stays so moist once it's cooked. This also makes it the go-to choice for fish and chips.

Good-quality cod is firm and fresh looking, and smells like the ocean. Always avoid fish that smells "fishy."

When it comes to storing fish, it's best to wrap the fillets in a damp paper towel and then again in plastic wrap. Next, place your pouches of fish in a shallow dish and cover them with a sealed bag of crushed ice. Chilling the fish fillets will help to keep them firm and fresh.

THE BEST FISH AND CHIPS YOU'VE EVER HAD: CRISPY BEER-BATTERED COD · **TWICE-COOKED HAND-CUT CHIPS** · TARTAR SAUCE FROM SCRATCH · **LEMON SALT**

I was eight or nine years old when I had my first taste of fish and chips. Until then, I wasn't big on fish. Then I went on a biking adventure with my mom, Louise. We took the ferry from Horseshoe Bay in Vancouver, British Columbia, to the Sunshine Coast and then biked to Gibsons, a picturesque little seaside town. After an afternoon of riding, I developed quite a hunger and Mom suggested we swing past the local fish and chips shop. I ended up devouring a newspaper cone full of fresh hand-cut chips and a crispy piece of beer-battered cod. Boy, was it good. Needless to say, I've never looked back.

Malt vinegar paired with delicately crispy beer-battered cod is truly magical. Throughout my culinary career, I've been fortunate enough to eat in some world-class restaurants. The food is amazing, but I always conclude that I love simple dishes just as much. Fish and chips is proof that simple food is the way forward.

If you can't find cod to make this main, try using halibut, haddock, or sole. {Serves 4}

[TIMING IS EVERYTHING]

Make Lemon Salt (can be made in advance and stored indefinitely) • Cut chips • Boil water and add chips • Prepare tartar sauce (can be made up to 1 week in advance and refrigerated) • Remove chips from water to dry • Prepare beer batter • Fry chips • Fry cod

CRISPY BEER-BATTERED COD

1 tsp active dry yeast
3 Tbsp warm (body-temperature) water
1 bottle beer, room temperature
1¼ cup flour, sifted
four 4 oz cod fillets (or cod fillets to equal 1½ lb total)
½ cup flour, for dusting
salt and pepper
Lemon Salt

To prepare beer batter, combine yeast and warm water in a medium bowl. Let stand about 5 minutes at room temperature; yeast should begin to foam slightly. Add beer and stir in flour. Mix should be about the consistency of pancake batter; adjust with additional flour or water if necessary.

Dust fillets with flour and season lightly with salt and pepper. Dip one at a time into batter and fry, in small batches, in 360°F oil until golden, about 5 to 6 minutes. Remove fillets with slotted spoon and drain on paper towels. Season fillets with Lemon Salt while still warm.

TWICE-COOKED HAND-CUT CHIPS

4 large russet potatoes
4 cups vegetable oil for frying (approximately)
1 Tbsp Lemon Salt

Peel and cut each potato into 9 thick, long chips. Bring a large pot of salted water to a rolling boil. Gently boil the potatoes for 4 to 6 minutes; they should be opaque, puffy, and slightly breaking up around the edges. Gently drain and spread out on a tray to dry out slightly.

Heat vegetable oil in a wide, deep pot to 360°F. Deep-fry potatoes until golden brown for 4 to 6 minutes. Remove using a slotted spoon and drain on paper towels. Season chips generously with Lemon Salt while still warm. Keep chips warm by placing them on a baking rack in a warm oven; this allows the air to circulate and helps keep them crispy. Keep the oil heated for the fish.

TARTAR SAUCE FROM SCRATCH

1 egg yolk
1 Tbsp Dijon mustard
juice of 1 lemon
1¼ cup vegetable oil
1 shallot, finely minced
3 Tbsp minced pickles
3 Tbsp chopped chives
2 Tbsp capers, drained and finely chopped
2 Tbsp chopped parsley
hot sauce
salt and pepper

Combine egg yolk, Dijon mustard, and lemon juice in a medium bowl. Using an immersion blender, blend in vegetable oil in a slow, steady stream. Fold in shallot, pickles, chives, capers, and parsley. Season to taste with hot sauce and salt and pepper.

LEMON SALT

zest of 1 lemon
½ cup flaky sea salt

Combine lemon zest and salt in a medium bowl and mix well. Spread on a tray or plate to dry out overnight.

C O R N

Corn is a wonderful and often underappreciated food. No truly classic French dishes include corn as it was once considered "feed" for animals. Now, corn is used in a wide range of products, from bourbon and whisky to flour and biofuel. Most importantly, it's great as an ingredient in a variety of dishes, or on its own.

There's really no comparison between canned or frozen corn and the fresh stuff. Corn thrives from May through September. It is ideally consumed within a day or two as its natural sugars begin turning to starch once it is picked.

The two most popular varieties of corn are Country Gentlemen (white corn), which is prized

THE ULTIMATE CLAM AND CORN CHOWDER · CHEDDAR CORN CAKES · JALAPEÑO CHIVE BUTTER

Chowder is a great way to showcase corn's sweet taste and crunchy texture. The soup gets its name from *chaudière*, the wide, deep pot it's traditionally cooked in. While the pot is French, the classic seafood soup is undisputedly from Boston. Similar versions are popular throughout Ireland and the east coast of Canada, where the soup's simple ingredients are abundant and cheap. The ingredients are so readily available, in fact, that chowder was once served to peasants and convicts.

This chowder is close to my heart, and brings all the things I love in life together in a bowl of warm, comforting heaven. Corn is beautiful in this soup, and works in harmony with most fish, but especially clams because they share a wonderful natural sweetness. Canned clams are great in this soup, but I like to use fresh ones too because they look so lovely and are, of course, delicious. The herbs in this chowder balance out its richness—I've used thyme here, but chives or parsley work well too. Keep in mind this soup only gets better with time, so this is a great make-ahead main.

In my world, it is a criminal offence punishable by death to serve a soup without some sort of top-tier bread, roll, bun, or biscuit. No exceptions, no trial. These biscuits are it: sharp cheddar, sweet corn, all good. {Serves 4}

THE ULTIMATE CLAM AND CORN CHOWDER

½ cup diced bacon
½ cup diced onion
½ cup diced carrot
½ cup diced celery
1 cup white wine
2 cups corn kernels
1 Tbsp butter
1 Tbsp flour
2½ cups milk
1 cup clam juice
1 cup diced potatoes
½ cup canned clams
2 sprigs thyme
2 bay leaves
salt and white pepper
1½ lb littleneck clams (optional)

In a large pot over medium-high heat, sauté bacon for 2 to 3 minutes, or until fat has rendered and bacon is crispy. Add onion and carrot and stir until slightly softened, about 2 to 3 minutes. Add celery and sauté another 2 to 3 minutes. Add white wine and simmer 2 to 3 minutes to allow liquid to reduce slightly.

Meanwhile, in a dry skillet, toast corn for 2 to 3 minutes, or until lightly charred and golden. Remove from heat.

Add butter and flour to wine mixture. Stir until butter has melted, about 1 to 2 minutes. Add milk, clam juice, potatoes, canned clams, thyme, bay leaves, and charred corn. Simmer, covered, about 15 to 20 minutes, or until potatoes are tender. Season soup with salt and white pepper.

Add littleneck clams to soup and cook until clams open, about 7 to 10 minutes.

CHEDDAR CORN CAKES

1¼ cup all-purpose flour
½ cup cornmeal
2 tsp baking powder
¾ tsp salt
⅓ cup cold butter, cut into ½-inch pieces
¾ cup blanched corn kernels
½ cup grated cheddar cheese
1 Tbsp chopped thyme
¾ cup milk
1 egg
1 Tbsp cayenne pepper

Preheat oven to 375°F.

In a large bowl, mix flour, cornmeal, baking powder, and salt. Add butter and mix with fingertips until mixture resembles coarse meal. Add corn, grated cheese, and thyme. Add milk and stir just until mixture comes together.

Turn dough out onto a lightly floured surface. Knead gently just until dough holds together. Roll dough out into a 9-inch round, about ¾-inch thick. Cut into 3-inch rounds with a biscuit cutter. Transfer rounds to a parchment-lined baking sheet.

In a small bowl, whisk egg. Brush each biscuit with egg and sprinkle with cayenne pepper. Bake in pre-heated oven for 15 to 20 minutes, or until golden brown.

JALAPEÑO CHIVE BUTTER

1 cup butter, softened
1 jalapeño, seeded and finely chopped
¼ cup chopped chives

In a medium bowl, combine all ingredients. Transfer to a small container and chill. Let stand 5 minutes at room temperature before serving.

51

CRAB

Crab is a delicate, sweet, and succulent shellfish of which there are over four thousand varieties. One of the most common is Dungeness crab, which is the pride of the Pacific coast. It has pale pink meat that is tender, sweet, and juicy. Crabs usually range from one to five pounds; a much larger variety, the king crab, usually weighs between five and fifteen pounds. King crab has chunky, sweet white meat laced with red. It's the muse for the imitation crabmeat found in a lot of sushi joints. Also known as Alaskan crab, king crab is incredibly expensive because Arctic fishing conditions are so harsh—working on a crab boat is one of the most dangerous jobs in the world.

CRAB CAKES WITH CRUNCHY CELERY
AND TART GREEN APPLE · GRILLED ARTICHOKES
WITH LEMON AND OLIVE OIL · BALSAMIC MARINATED
TOMATOES · LEMON-CAPER AIOLI

C rab cakes are delicious and easy to put together, but keep in mind that crab has a delicate, slightly sweet taste that can be overpowered by too many strong flavours. I love this recipe; unlike many other crab cakes, this one really tastes like crab. Frozen or canned chunked crab works best for this recipe. If you use crab legs, make sure you remove all bits of shell.

The other highlight of these crab cakes is the Granny Smith apple. The apple's natural sweetness, light flavour, and crispness pairs beautifully with the crab. Apple also balances the cakes with its tart-

ness and adds to the moist texture brought by the sour cream and mayonnaise. Tarragon (one of my top three favourite herbs) complements the apple's flavour with its unique licorice taste.

I don't even attempt crab cakes without a great dip in mind—they need it. This one is simple, light, and tangy. The capers, which are actually salt-cured flower buds, give it a nice edge. The grilled artichokes and marinated tomatoes both bring fresh, delicate flavours to the table—the perfect sides for my crab cakes. {Serves 4}

CRAB CAKES WITH CRUNCHY CELERY AND TART GREEN APPLE

2 Tbsp olive oil (divided)
½ medium onion, finely chopped
1 stalk celery, finely chopped
2 Tbsp white wine
1½ lb lump crabmeat, drained
    and picked over
1 Granny Smith apple, peeled
    and grated
¼ cup mayonnaise
¼ cup sour cream
¼ cup finely chopped chives
2 Tbsp finely chopped tarragon
½ tsp cayenne
1 egg yolk
1 cup breadcrumbs (divided)
salt and pepper

Preheat oven to 375°F.

In a skillet, heat 1 Tbsp olive oil over low heat. Add onion and celery and cook gently for 3 to 4 minutes, or until vegetables are soft and translucent. Add white wine and cook slowly over medium heat, covered, until vegetables are tender. Remove from heat and set aside.

In a large bowl, combine crabmeat, apple, mayonnaise, sour cream, chives, tarragon, cayenne, and egg yolk. Add ⅓ cup of breadcrumbs. Add onion and celery mixture and combine well. Season with salt and pepper. If mixture does not hold together, add more breadcrumbs.

Place remaining ⅔ cup of bread-crumbs into a large shallow dish. Divide crab mixture into 8 portions. Form crab cakes into 2-inch rounds about 1 inch thick. Dip the top and bottom of each crab cake into bread-crumbs. Set on a baking sheet.

In a non-stick pan, heat remaining 1 Tbsp of oil over medium-high heat. Add 4 crab cakes and cook for 2 to 3 minutes, or until golden brown. Flip crab cakes and sear another 1 minute. Transfer crab cakes to baking sheet. Repeat with remaining crab cakes.

Place baking sheet in preheated oven and bake for 6 to 7 minutes, or until crab cakes are heated through.

GRILLED ARTICHOKES WITH LEMON AND OLIVE OIL

¼ cup white vinegar
2 Tbsp salt
4 large artichokes, quartered
    (or 8 small artichokes, halved),
    stems trimmed, and outer
    leaves removed
¼ cup olive oil
juice of ½ lemon
1 garlic clove, finely chopped
salt and pepper

In a large pot with a lid, bring 8 cups of water to a boil. Add white vinegar and salt. Add artichokes and cover. Continue boiling for 15 to 20 minutes, or until tender. Drain artichokes.

Preheat barbecue or indoor grill to medium heat.

In a medium bowl, combine olive oil, lemon juice, and garlic. Add artichokes and toss gently with dressing. Season with salt and pepper.

Wrap artichokes in aluminum foil and place on preheated grill. Cook for 8 to 10 minutes, or until slightly charred. Serve with Balsamic Marinated Tomatoes.

BALSAMIC MARINATED TOMATOES

2 cups cherry tomatoes, sliced in
    half, or 2 cups chopped Roma
    tomatoes
2 Tbsp good-quality olive oil
1 Tbsp chopped chives (or basil)
1 Tbsp balsamic vinegar
salt and pepper

In a medium bowl, combine toma-toes, olive oil, chives, and balsamic vinegar. Season with salt and pepper.

LEMON-CAPER AIOLI

½ cup sour cream
½ cup mayonnaise
2 Tbsp chopped capers
zest of 1 lemon
juice of ½ lemon
salt and pepper

In a medium bowl, combine sour cream, mayonnaise, chopped capers, lemon zest, and lemon juice. Season with salt and pepper.

55

DUCK

It might not be the first thing that comes to mind when you're wondering what to make for dinner, but duck is so delicious and easy to cook it's always a great option. Although duck breast has a fairly thick layer of fat, the meat itself is actually fairly lean. If you simply score the fat in a fine criss-cross pattern, it will melt away as it cooks.

Just be sure not to cut so deep that you cut into the actual flesh of the duck breast.

Duck breast should be cooked slowly to prevent it from drying out. Aim for medium-rare to medium, as anything else will leave the meat either chewy or tough. To achieve a nice crispy skin, place the scored-fat side of the duck down in

PAN-FRIED DUCK BREAST WITH ORANGE, THYME, AND JUNIPER RUB · ROSEMARY-ROASTED PLUMS · ROASTED CELERIAC · ORANGE RELISH · FRISÉE SALAD WITH SHALLOT, RED WINE VINEGAR, AND WALNUTS

Duck has always been associated with a certain level of luxury, which can make cooking it at home quite intimidating. I used to only really eat duck at high-end restaurants, and rarely at home. Duck, however, is quickly becoming more accessible and sought after by the home chef, and the truth is that it couldn't be easier to cook.

Duck and orange is a classic combination. In this main, the meat's rich, full flavour pairs particularly well with the tart sweetness of orange in both the

quick, effortless ways to get heaps of flavour.

Like most game meats and birds, duck works especially well with fruits. My rosemary-accented roasted plums bring just the right level of sweetness to this savoury dish. I've always loved savoury dishes that incorporate sweetness. All chefs I have worked under have picked this out in my cooking and attributed it to the fact that I'm still young and have a sweet tooth. I think I just like it because it's good! {Serves 4}

[TIMING IS EVERYTHING]

Pat duck with spice rub and refrigerate • Prepare relish • Prepare salad dressing,
and toast walnuts • Cook duck • Roast celeriac and plums • Dress salad • Serve
sliced duck overtop roasted celeriac and plums and drizzle with plum reduction
• Serve relish and salad on the side

PAN-FRIED DUCK BREAST WITH ORANGE, THYME, AND JUNIPER RUB

4 duck breasts
1 Tbsp black pepper
zest of 1 orange
2 tsp crushed juniper berries
⅓ cup chopped parsley
1 Tbsp thyme leaves
1 tsp coarse sea salt

Lightly score skin side of breasts. Combine black pepper, orange zest, juniper berries, parsley, and thyme in a small bowl and mix well. Pat firmly onto flesh side of duck breasts. Let sit in the refrigerator for 30 minutes.

Preheat oven to 400°F.

Let duck breasts stand at room temperature for at least 10 minutes. Season generously on flesh sides with coarse sea salt. Place duck breasts skin side down in a large, cold, ovenproof skillet and cook slowly over medium heat until fat renders and skin becomes crispy and golden, about 7 to 8 minutes. Drain pan of excess fat as needed; reserve 2 Tbsp of duck fat for the Roasted Celeriac. Finish cooking in oven about 4 to 5 minutes. Remove from heat and let rest at least 10 minutes in a warm place. Thinly slice against grain just before serving.

ROSEMARY-ROASTED PLUMS

4 large plums, halved and pits removed
2 Tbsp sugar
pinch of salt
2 sprigs rosemary
1 Tbsp olive oil
½ cup port
1 Tbsp butter

Preheat oven to 400°F.

In a medium bowl, combine plums, sugar, salt, rosemary, and olive oil, and toss to coat. Arrange mixture in an ovenproof pan or shallow baking dish and roast until plums are soft and jammy, about 30 minutes.

Transfer plums to a serving dish, leaving the liquid in the pan. Deglaze plum juices with port and transfer to a pot. Bring to a simmer on the stovetop, reducing volume by half. Remove from heat and swirl in butter. Season sauce with salt and pepper. Set aside.

ROASTED CELERIAC

4 small celeriac bulbs
2 Tbsp duck fat (reserved from rendering duck breasts) or olive oil
1 Tbsp butter
2 sprigs thyme
salt and pepper

Preheat oven to 400°F.

Peel celeriac and cube into bite-sized pieces. Heat duck fat in a large ovenproof skillet. Sear celeriac until light golden on all sides; add butter and thyme sprigs. Season with salt and pepper and roast in oven until outsides are golden and insides are tender, about 20 minutes.

ORANGE RELISH

1 large orange
3 Tbsp sugar
2 Tbsp white wine vinegar
salt and pepper

Peel orange, leaving white pith behind. Blanch peels briefly in boiling water; drain and roughly chop. Trim off and discard white pith from orange. Cut orange into small pieces and combine with chopped peel, sugar, and white wine vinegar in a small saucepan. Simmer gently until liquid cooks down and relish becomes slightly syrupy, about 5 to 6 minutes. Season with salt and pepper.

FRISÉE SALAD WITH SHALLOT, RED WINE VINEGAR, AND WALNUTS

1 small shallot, finely minced
2 Tbsp red wine vinegar
4 Tbsp olive oil
salt and pepper
1 head frisée, washed well and dark, tough outer leaves trimmed
¼ cup walnuts, toasted and roughly chopped

Combine shallot, red wine vinegar, and olive oil in a medium mixing bowl. Season with salt and pepper. Tear or snip the frisée into bite-sized pieces. Add to bowl and toss well. Top with walnuts.

FIGS

Figs originated in Europe, Asia, and Africa, where they are often considered a symbol of prosperity and good faith. Spanish and Portuguese missionaries introduced the fruit to North America in the 17th century, and gave the popular mission fig its name. There are hundreds of varieties of the small fruit, in many different colours including white, green, pink, purple, and even black. They all share a tender skin and soft flesh loaded with tiny edible seeds.

Store fresh figs in the fridge and gently cover them with a paper towel to slow the ripening process. Ripe figs are extremely soft and delicate; handle them carefully to avoid bruising and damage.

GRILLED CHICKEN, FIG, AND BRIE
CIABATTA WITH HOMEMADE AIOLI · SWEET
POTATO FRIES WITH SMOKED PAPRIKA

As a young cook, I was often told that every chef's individual flair comes from his or her own creativity combined with the styles of the chefs he or she has worked under. When I go out to restaurants, I'm always on the hunt for ideas and inspirations. A couple of years ago, I ate at a restaurant in Vancouver, British Columbia, my hometown, and tried a dish that incorporated poorly cooked chicken and dried figs. The food wasn't great, but the idea had potential. I got to thinking about what a nice combination the mild flavour of grilled chicken would be with fresh figs and quickly got to work. This sandwich became a simple, elegant lunch. Grilled chicken topped with sweet and tender figs, creamy brie, earthy walnuts, and peppery arugula on a toasted ciabatta with homemade garlic aioli? Count me in! My little trick of rubbing the ciabatta with a clove of garlic is a great one, and it can be applied to any toasted breads to make the easiest garlic toast ever! *{Serves 4}*

[TIMING IS EVERYTHING]

Grill chicken breasts • Prepare aioli and refrigerate (can be made up to 1 week in advance and refrigerated) • Cut sweet potato fries and bake • Assemble sandwiches • Move fries to oven's bottom shelf and broil sandwiches • Top with arugula

GRILLED CHICKEN, FIG, AND BRIE CIABATTA WITH HOMEMADE AIOLI

Chicken

2 chicken breasts, skinless
  and boneless
olive oil
salt and pepper

Homemade aioli

1 large egg yolk
pinch of salt
pinch of pepper
juice of 1 lemon
1 cup olive oil
2 small cloves garlic
dash of hot sauce (optional)

Sandwich

4 slices ciabatta bread, ½ inch thick
1 garlic clove, cut in half
¼ cup toasted walnut halves
  (about 8 pieces)
4 fresh figs, sliced ¼ inch thick
4 slices brie, about ¼ inch thick
½ cup arugula, washed and dried
olive oil
salt and pepper
2 tsp honey (optional)

Preheat barbecue or indoor grill to medium-high heat.

To prepare chicken, season breasts with olive oil and salt and pepper. Grill over medium-high heat until done, about 6 to 8 minutes. Let rest before carving into ½-inch-thick slices. Set aside.

To prepare aioli, combine egg yolk, salt, pepper, and lemon juice in a medium-sized measuring cup or tall glass. Using a hand-held immersion blender, blend the ingredients while adding the oil in a slow stream. Blend in garlic and hot sauce. Season with more salt and lemon juice, if necessary. Set aside.

To assemble sandwich, turn broiler on. Toast bread until light golden; rub each slice with cut side of garlic clove and season with salt. Spread aioli generously on each slice. Top each slice with chicken, walnuts, and figs. Place brie on top and broil until cheese melts. Remove from oven and place on serving plates. Place a loose handful of arugula on top of melted cheese. Dress lightly with olive oil, honey, and salt and pepper.

SWEET POTATO FRIES WITH SMOKED PAPRIKA

3 large sweet potatoes, peeled
  and each cut into 6 wedges
3 Tbsp olive oil
pinch of cayenne
pinch of smoked paprika
salt and pepper
1 green onion, chopped
juice of 1 lime

Preheat oven to 375°F.

In a large bowl, combine sweet potato wedges, olive oil, cayenne, smoked paprika, and salt and pepper. Toss well to combine. Arrange on baking sheet and bake, turning over occasionally until cooked through and golden brown, about 20 minutes. Toss with green onion and bake another 1 minute. Squeeze lime juice over fries and season with salt and pepper.

FLANK STEAK

Flank steak is a unique cut of beef because it can be slowly braised, lightly seared, or grilled. A lean-cut flank steak should be cooked to medium-rare or medium (when grilling or searing). Cooking it any further can make it tough. To ensure a great steak with loads of flavour, go for a top-quality

well-aged piece of meat with just enough marbled fat throughout to keep it juicy.

Let your steak rest! This means letting your steak hang out on a cutting board or plate for five to eight minutes after it's cooked. It gives the meat the opportunity to relax, which results in a

65

RED WINE–MARINATED FLANK
STEAK · **CARAMELIZED ONIONS** · ROASTED
POTATOES WITH THYME · **ARUGULA SALAD**
WITH BALSAMIC VINEGAR

A simply grilled steak is something special, and this version is no exception. I buy flank steak to cook at home because it's a reasonably priced cut with great flavour. In this recipe it's lightly grilled and some great flavour is added through a red wine marinade.

If you're a regular viewer of *The Main* you've probably heard me explain all too often the reason we marinate meat, poultry, and fish. Here it is again. We marinate, of course, to impart flavour and to tenderize the meat. In this case, the acidity in the wine and red wine vinegar tenderizes the flank steak. The wine becomes sweeter as the marinade reduces into a sauce, and the meat's robust, bold taste combines beautifully with the green peppercorns, garlic, and thyme. The marinade also helps keep the steak juicy as it grills.

Roasted potatoes and a simple salad on the side make this a wonderfully rustic main. This is what I go for when I want a delicious, uncomplicated dinner. {Serves 4}

Marinate flank steak • Prepare and cook caramelized onions and roasted potatoes • Grill steak and set aside to rest • Reduce marinade • Prepare vinaigrette and dress salad • Divide potatoes evenly among plates • Put steak on plates and top with onions • Spoon reduced marinade sauce over steak and onions • Arrange salad on side

RED WINE–MARINATED FLANK STEAK

one 28–30 oz flank steak
pepper
1 cup red wine
4 cloves garlic, finely chopped
2 shallots, diced
3–4 sprigs thyme
1 Tbsp green peppercorns
1 Tbsp red wine vinegar
coarse salt
1 cup beef stock
2 Tbsp cold butter, diced

Lightly score flank steak in a criss-cross pattern on both sides and season well with pepper.

Combine red wine, garlic, shallots, thyme, peppercorns, and red wine vinegar in a shallow baking dish. Marinate steak in the refrigerator for at least 60 minutes; overnight is ideal.

Preheat barbecue or indoor grill to high. Remove steak from marinade (reserving marinade), pat dry, and season both sides generously with coarse salt. Grill each side for 3 to 4 minutes; remove from heat and let rest for at least 5 minutes before cutting steaks against the grain into four equal pieces. If desired, carve each portion against the grain into thinner slices.

Pour marinade and beef stock into a large, wide saucepan and bring to a simmer. Reduce volume by half; liquid should have a saucy consistency. Reduce heat to low and gently swirl in cold butter, one piece at a time. Adjust seasoning with salt and pepper.

CARAMELIZED ONIONS

2 medium red onions
1 Tbsp butter
1 Tbsp olive oil
2 Tbsp roughly cubed pancetta
1 bay leaf
salt

Trim tops and root ends of onions and peel off papery skin. Cut each onion in half, going from top to root end. Place onions flat side down and make an angled cut to remove core. Thinly slice along grain.

Heat butter and olive oil in a medium heavy-bottomed pot set over medium-high heat. When butter is melted, add onions, pancetta, bay leaf, and salt. Stir occasionally until onions soften and start to colour, about 8 to 10 minutes. Lower heat slightly and stir more frequently as onions darken to prevent burning. Onions are done when very soft and deep golden brown. Remove from heat and keep warm.

ROASTED POTATOES WITH THYME

4 medium potatoes, cut in
  ¼-inch slices
1 small onion, cut in ¼-inch slices
3 Tbsp olive oil
1 sprig thyme
salt and pepper

Preheat oven to 475°F.

Toss sliced potatoes and onions in olive oil and spread on an ovenproof dish or baking sheet in a single layer. Add thyme and season generously with salt and pepper. Roast in hot oven, turning slices over if necessary, until golden, about 10 to 12 minutes. Remove from heat and keep warm.

ARUGULA SALAD WITH BALSAMIC VINEGAR

4 cups baby arugula, washed
  and dried
2 tsp extra virgin olive oil
1 tsp balsamic vinegar
salt and pepper

Gently toss arugula with olive oil and balsamic vinegar, and season with salt and pepper.

FONTINA CHEESE

Fondue is the perfect sharing dish—a pot of melting cheese accompanied by an array of meats, fish, vegetables, crackers, and breads to dip. Now a retro classic, fondue has been enjoyed throughout the Alps for centuries. It is most commonly associated with Switzerland, but many

other countries have their own versions, which feature cheeses like Gruyère, Emmenthal, Beaufort, Taleggio, Edam, and Gouda. The Italians call fondue *fonduta*, and typically make it from fontina cheese—an Italian cow's milk cheese that has been produced in the Aosta Valley since the 12th century

FONTINA FONDUTA · CRISPY POTATOES · GRILLED STRIPLOIN STEAK, ASPARAGUS, AND MUSHROOMS · SALSA VERDE · TOASTED BREAD

The key to a successful *fonduta* is soaking the fontina in milk before melting it over a double boiler with butter and egg yolks. I like to season the fontina with salt and truffle oil because it's such a mild cheese. Its subtle flavour and creamy texture are also enhanced by the other elements of this main: the crispy potatoes are a great contrast, the mushrooms offer a pungent earthiness, the asparagus brings a nice fresh crunch, and the tangy bite of the Salsa Verde (green salsa) enhances the cheese's herby notes. My salsa is a simple combination of fresh herbs, anchovies, mustard, and vinegar, which can be puréed or chopped into a rough pesto-like consistency. I love the fact that it can be used as a condiment, dressing, sauce, or dip. My favourite way to eat this main is by making little sandwiches out of all this great gear, and then dipping them in the good stuff. *{Serves 4}*

[TIMING IS EVERYTHING]
Prepare Salsa Verde (can be made up to 2 days in advance and refrigerated) •
Soak fontina • Cook potatoes • Begin cooking fonduta • Grill steak, mushrooms,
and asparagus (serve at room temperature) • Finish fonduta and toast bread

FONTINA FONDUTA

14 oz Italian fontina, cut into
   small cubes
1 cup whole milk
3 egg yolks
1 tsp white truffle oil
salt
1 clove garlic, peeled

In a medium bowl, soak fontina in
whole milk for 2 hours, or until softened. Drain cheese, reserving milk.

In a double boiler, whisk egg yolks
and reserved whole milk together over
medium heat for 2 to 4 minutes. Add
fontina and cook, stirring occasionally,
until completely melted.

Season with truffle oil and salt and
cook for another 5 minutes. Do not
allow the mixture to boil or it will
separate. Meanwhile, rub the inside
of a fondue pot with peeled clove
of garlic. Transfer cheese mixture to
fondue pot.

CRISPY POTATOES

10–12 new potatoes, peeled and cut
   into 1-inch pieces
½ cup vegetable oil
salt

Bring a large pot of salted water to
a boil. Add potatoes and cook 7 to
10 minutes, or until tender. Drain,
being careful not to break up any
pieces, and lay on a sheet pan to cool.

In a large non-stick skillet, heat oil
over medium heat. Add potatoes in
batches and cook until golden brown

on all sides, 5 to 6 minutes. Drain on
paper towels and sprinkle with salt.
Keep warm.

GRILLED STRIPLOIN STEAK, ASPARAGUS, AND MUSHROOMS

two 12 oz striploin steaks
salt and pepper
1 bunch asparagus, ends trimmed
12 button or cremini mushrooms,
   wiped clean
3 Tbsp olive oil

Pat steaks dry and season with salt
and pepper.

In a large bowl, toss asparagus and
mushrooms with olive oil, and salt
and pepper.

Preheat barbecue or indoor grill to
medium-high heat.

Cook steak to desired doneness,
about 6 to 8 minutes per side for
medium. Let rest 5 minutes and cut
into 1-inch cubes. While steak is rest-
ing, grill asparagus and mushrooms
5 to 7 minutes, or until tender.

SALSA VERDE

1 cup chopped parsley, stems
   included
6 anchovies, finely chopped
2 Tbsp finely chopped capers
1 Tbsp red wine vinegar
2 tsp Dijon mustard
½ clove garlic, minced
2–3 drops Tabasco sauce
⅓ cup olive oil

In a medium bowl, mix parsley, anchovies, capers, red wine vinegar, Dijon
mustard, garlic, and Tabasco sauce.
Add olive oil and stir to combine.

TOASTED BREAD

1 loaf Italian country bread
   or baguette

Slice bread into ½-inch slices. Toast on
grill 2 to 3 minutes per side, or until
golden and crispy.

GARLIC

What would cooking be without the pungent taste of garlic? Garlic is a part of the onion family and comes in many varieties including the common Silver-skin, wild, Elephant, and Artichoke. When you're buying garlic, look for bulbs that are tightly formed and completely covered with layers of papery skin. Garlic should be stored in the pantry or on the countertop, not in the fridge. If the cloves have small green shoots in the centre, they've seen better times and it's best to part ways.

Roasted garlic is dead easy to make and great as an addition to breads, potato purées, dressings,

and sauces, or as a spread on its own. Take a bulb of garlic and cut the top off, just so the cloves are visible. Place the bulb onto a small piece of aluminum foil and then hit it up with a drizzle of olive oil, some salt, and freshly ground black pepper. You can also add a sprig of thyme or rosemary for a subtle herb flavour. Bundle the foil around the garlic bulb and roast it at 350°F until it's soft, about 45 minutes. Allow it to cool slightly, then remove the garlic from the foil and squeeze out the cloves from the entire bulb.

MY FAVOURITE ROAST CHICKEN WITH FORTY CLOVES OF GARLIC · ARUGULA BREAD SALAD WITH TOASTED PINE NUTS AND CURRANTS · SIMPLY GRILLED OYSTER MUSHROOMS

I cannot stress how incredible this roast chicken is. The brine makes for the most flavourful, juicy, succulent, and mouthwatering meat you'll ever have the pleasure of wiping off your face. I developed this recipe based on an idea from Justin, a great chef and friend. Not only do the forty cloves of garlic bring a certain "wow factor" to this main, but they also have an amazing flavour. As I was working on the recipe, I found that by using garlic cooked in a variety of ways I could incorporate its wonderful flavour without overpowering the dish or leaving the person consuming it with dragon breath.

The garlic in the brine has a nice mellow flavour once cooked. The garlic placed under the skin of the chicken caramelizes, becoming sweet and crisp. Finally, the two whole heads of roasted garlic beside the chicken infuse the bird with aromatic flavour. The garlic itself becomes sweet and buttery when roasted.

Garlic lovers rejoice—this main's for you. {Serves 4}

MY FAVOURITE ROAST CHICKEN WITH FORTY CLOVES OF GARLIC

Brine

3 cups water
3 cups white wine
1 stalk celery, roughly chopped
½ onion, roughly chopped
10 cloves garlic, peeled and crushed
2 tsp whole white peppercorns
6 bay leaves
3–4 parsley stems
1 sprig thyme
¼ cup salt
¼ cup sugar

Chicken

one 3–3½ lb chicken
4 Tbsp softened butter (divided)
2 cloves garlic, thinly sliced
4 sprigs parsley
2 sprigs thyme
1 onion, sliced into ¼-inch rings
coarse salt and pepper
2 heads garlic, tops cut off
  lengthways
¼ cup olive oil

To prepare brine, combine all ingredients in pot large enough to fit a whole chicken and bring to a boil. Let cool to room temperature. Submerge chicken in brine, weighing down with a plate if necessary, and let sit overnight in fridge.

Preheat oven to 400°F.

Remove chicken from brine and pat dry. Strain brine, reserving celery, onion, garlic, herbs, and spices. Smear 2 Tbsp of butter under breast skin. Tuck sliced garlic under skin as well.

Tuck fresh herbs and reserved celery, onion, and garlic inside before trussing chicken. Rub remaining butter into skin and season generously all over with coarse salt and pepper. Arrange onion slices in a lightly oiled roasting pan. Place chicken on top. Toss heads of garlic in olive oil and arrange beside chicken.

Roast in oven, basting occasionally, for about 60 minutes, or until juices run clear. Allow chicken to rest for at least 15 minutes before carving.

ARUGULA BREAD SALAD WITH TOASTED PINE NUTS AND CURRANTS

3 Tbsp currants, soaked in ¼ cup sweet wine (Vin Santo or late harvest wine)
4 cups arugula, washed and dried
½ loaf focaccia, cut into 1-inch cubes and lightly toasted (about 3 cups)
¼ cup olive oil
2 Tbsp red wine vinegar
¼ cup toasted pine nuts
salt and pepper

Drain soaked currants and reserve wine. Combine arugula, cubed bread, and drained currants in a medium bowl. Gently toss with olive oil, 1 Tbsp of reserved sweet wine, and vinegar. Top with pine nuts and season with salt and pepper.

SIMPLY GRILLED OYSTER MUSHROOMS

3 cups oyster mushrooms
3 Tbsp olive oil (divided)
salt and pepper

Preheat barbecue or indoor grill to high heat.

Trim any woody stems off the mushrooms. Drizzle mushrooms with 2 Tbsp olive oil and season lightly with salt and pepper. Grill mushrooms until lightly charred and crispy in places, about 2 to 3 minutes each side. Transfer to a plate or tray and keep warm until serving. Finish by drizzling remaining 1 Tbsp olive oil over mushrooms before serving.

75

GNOCCHI

Gnocchi is the Italian word for "dumpling." Simple, hearty, and delicious, gnocchi are usually made from boiled, milled potatoes that are bound with flour, and sometimes egg, to form a dough. Other additions can include cheese, spinach, and herbs. Fresh gnocchi is cooked in boiling water like pasta,

although it takes far less time to cook—when the gnocchi begin to float, they're done.

Gnocchi can vary in size and shape, but they're often curved into a half moon because this allows a sauce to stick to them better. Gnocchi can also be rolled against a fork or a gnocchi paddle, which

creates small grooves in the dumplings where
sauce can adhere more easily.

Making gnocchi is easy and a lot of fun. It's a

HOMEMADE GNOCCHI IN A CREAMY GORGONZOLA SAUCE · GRILLED RADICCHIO WITH BALSAMIC VINEGAR · PEAR AND WALNUT SALAD

Making gnocchi, or any pasta, from scratch has a wonderfully back-to-basics feel. Even in the midst of a dinner rush in a hot, stressful restaurant kitchen, making gnocchi instantly transports me to a happy place. It's therapeutic and relaxing. In London's La Trompette restaurant, we used to make gnocchi and fresh pasta every day. My colleague Monty and I would make heaps of the little dumplings in the back of the kitchen with the music blaring. Good times.

In classic Italian style, this recipe showcases humble, everyday ingredients in a way that makes them rich and decadent. Once cooked, the tiny, tender gnocchi are enveloped in a rich and creamy Gorgonzola sauce. The rich sauce is perfectly balanced by the radicchio's refreshing bitterness and the mild sweetness of the balsamic vinegar. With a heavier main like this, I like to keep things light on the side, so I've made a simple, refreshing salad with pears and walnuts. {Serves 4}

HOMEMADE GNOCCHI IN A CREAMY GORGONZOLA SAUCE

Gnocchi

1½ lb russet potatoes (about
  3 medium)
1 egg
¼ cup grated Parmesan
¼ cup fresh ricotta
1½ cups flour, plus ¼ cup for dusting
pinch of nutmeg
salt and pepper

Sauce

½ cup whipping cream (35%)
¼ cup crumbled Gorgonzola
juice of ½ lemon

Put potatoes in a medium pot and fill with cold water to cover. Season cooking water with salt (it should taste like the sea) and bring to a boil; lower heat and simmer until potatoes are tender but not overcooked, about 10 to 12 minutes. Drain and allow to dry out slightly. While still warm, peel skin off potatoes, cut into quarters, and push through a ricer or food mill. Gently combine riced potatoes with egg, Parmesan, ricotta, flour, nutmeg, salt, and pepper, being careful not to overmix. On a floured board, divide dough into 6 pieces and roll each piece into a ¾-inch-thick log. Cut each log into ½-inch-long pieces. If desired, roll each piece on the back of a fork to create ridges. Lay out cut pieces on a lightly floured tray.

To cook, bring a large pot of salted water to a boil. Boil in batches, dropping in a few at a time; gnocchi are ready when they float to the surface, about 4 to 5 minutes. Remove with a slotted spoon onto a lightly greased tray.

For the sauce, bring cream to a simmer in a heavy, medium saucepan over medium heat. Add Gorgonzola, whisking until melted. Just before serving, whisk in lemon juice. To assemble dish, add cooked, drained gnocchi to saucepan and toss to coat.

GRILLED RADICCHIO WITH BALSAMIC VINEGAR

1 clove garlic, very finely minced
2 Tbsp balsamic vinegar
3 Tbsp olive oil, plus extra
  for drizzling
2 heads radicchio, halved
salt and pepper

Preheat barbecue or indoor grill to high heat.

Combine garlic, balsamic vinegar, and olive oil; toss well with radicchio to coat. Season very generously with salt and pepper. Grill until lightly charred, about 3 to 5 minutes. Transfer to a bowl and cover with plastic wrap; this will allow radicchio to soften slightly. Dress with additional extra virgin olive oil before serving.

PEAR AND WALNUT SALAD

1 small head frisée, tough green
  outer leaves removed
1 ripe Bosc pear, cut into
  bite-sized pieces
¼ cup walnut halves, toasted
1 Tbsp olive oil
2 tsp white wine vinegar
salt and pepper

Cut or rip frisée into bite-sized pieces; put in a medium bowl. Add pear and walnuts. Drizzle with olive oil and vinegar; toss gently and season with salt and pepper.

GOAT CHEESE

France, Spain, Portugal, England, Greece, and Italy are some of the greatest cheese-producing countries in the world, and all of them manufacture cheeses made from goat's milk. There are numerous styles of goat cheese, or *chèvre* (French for "goat"), ranging in flavour from mild and soft to strong and tangy. They are all unique and delicious—try as many as you can!

Although some varieties of goat cheese are richer, thicker, and creamier than cheeses made from cow's milk, they often have less fat, calories, and cholesterol. Eat up the healthy choice! Goat

CLASSIC COTTAGE PIE·IRISH
PEAS AND CABBAGE

I began my cooking career at the tender age of 13 and was privileged enough to sample the occasional tenderloin or striploin steak. Lucky, I know. Before that, though, I ate strictly at home, where it was all about the ground beef. Mom used to make a pretty bang-up meat sauce, which was ladled over thoroughly overcooked spaghetti and doused with powdered "Parmesan cheese" (purists would kill me for calling it Parmesan, but it was good). Ground beef was the go-to meat for our family. I still like to cook with it—it's tasty and cheap, and freezes well. Ground chuck, round, or sirloin are all great choices for my Classic Cottage Pie. They're loaded with flavour and relatively lean, making them a healthier choice. Although they're on the pricy side for ground beef, they are far more affordable than any whole cut. If you can, go all out.

It's worth noting that this recipe requires *cooking out* the sauce. The term is often used to describe the process of cooking out the "raw" taste, usually of white flour, when making a gravy or sauce. As the flour cooks, it blends into the other ingredients. {Serves 4}

[TIMING IS EVERYTHING]

Boil potatoes • Prepare pie filling • When potatoes are tender, assemble pie and add topping • Bake pie • Prepare Irish Peas and Cabbage

CLASSIC COTTAGE PIE

Filling

4 Tbsp vegetable oil (divided)
1 lb ground beef
1 cup red wine
2 tsp butter
¾ cup diced onion (about
  ½ an onion)
2 cups diced carrot (about
  2 medium)
1 cup diced celery (about 1 stalk)
2 cloves garlic, minced
1 heaping Tbsp tomato paste
2 Tbsp flour
2½ cups beef stock
1 sprig rosemary
1 sprig thyme
1 bay leaf
salt and pepper

Potatoes

7 medium cooking potatoes, peeled
  and quartered
3 cloves garlic, crushed
¼ cup whipping cream (35%)
⅓ cup butter
pepper
¼ cup grated Parmesan

Assembly

extra grated Parmesan
2 Tbsp butter, cut into small cubes
salt and pepper
¼ cup breadcrumbs (optional)

For the filling, heat 2 Tbsp vegetable oil in a large saucepan over medium-high heat. Add ground beef. Allow excess liquid to bubble away; stir and cook until meat is well browned and crispy, about 8 to 10 minutes. Drain excess fat using a colander and set ground beef aside. Deglaze pot with red wine, scraping up browned bits, and allow to reduce slightly.

In a separate large pan, heat remaining 2 Tbsp vegetable oil and butter over medium-high heat. Add onion, carrots, and celery; cook until golden, about 5 to 7 minutes. Add garlic, stir briefly, and add tomato paste. Brown tomato paste slightly and sprinkle in flour. Cook out (see recipe introduction) for 1 to 2 minutes. Add the reduced red wine from deglazing beef, scraping up crispy brown bits from bottom of pan. Add beef stock, rosemary, thyme, and bay leaf. Return browned meat to saucepan. Simmer, covered, for 20 to 25 minutes. Remove lid and continue cooking for another 10 minutes; liquid will reduce and thicken. Remove rosemary, thyme, and bay leaf. Season well with salt and pepper. Set aside until ready to assemble pie.

Put quartered potatoes and crushed garlic in a medium pot. Fill pot with cold water just to cover potatoes; season cooking water well with salt (it should taste like the sea) and bring to a boil. Boil over medium-high heat until potatoes are tender but not overdone, about 15 to 20 minutes. Strain potatoes; allow to dry out slightly in colander before returning to pot. Add whipping cream, butter, pepper, Parmesan, and more salt if necessary. Roughly mash with fork or potato masher.

To assemble the cottage pie, preheat oven to 400°F. Spoon filling into the bottom of a 10-inch round casserole dish. Top with mashed potatoes. Grate Parmesan on top and dot surface evenly with butter. Season with salt and pepper and sprinkle breadcrumbs overtop. Bake on middle rack until top is golden and filling is warmed through, about 20 to 25 minutes. Let stand for a few minutes before serving.

IRISH PEAS AND CABBAGE

1 Tbsp vegetable oil
2 strips bacon, roughly diced
½ small onion, sliced
½ head small Savoy cabbage, core
  removed and thinly sliced
2 cups frozen sweet peas
1 Tbsp butter
salt and pepper

Heat vegetable oil in a medium saucepan over medium-high heat. Sauté bacon until light golden. Add sliced onion and sauté until onion is translucent and just starting to colour. Add cabbage and sweat, cooking down until cabbage softens, about 5 minutes. Blanch peas in a separate pot of boiling salted water. Drain and add to cabbage mixture. Add butter and fold to coat lightly. Season with salt and pepper.

87

GROUND SIRLOIN

Ground sirloin is some of the tastiest, leanest ground beef out there. It tends to be slightly pricier than other ground cuts, but only nominally, and the bang-up flavour is well worth the extra dime. Ground sirloin is just 10 percent fat, a third of the fat content of regular ground beef. This makes it essential not to overcook ground sirloin as it can dry out quite easily.

Ideally ground beef should be purchased freshly ground from a reputable butcher and eaten within a day. The ultimate is finding a butcher who will grind it up just as you order it, as freshly ground

MY WORLD FAMOUS BURGER · HOMEMADE BBQ SAUCE · CABBAGE-CELERIAC COLESLAW · POUTINE WITH HOMEMADE GRAVY AND DOUBLE-SMOKED BACON

It's a shame what's happened to the hamburger. A quality backyard hero became a staple of the fast-food industry. Well, the great burger is back and no one can make it better than you can at home with this recipe. It's been a long time in the making—from watching my parents meticulously preparing burgers for summer barbecues to spending ten years in professional kitchens.

When it come to the meat, it's wise to choose a good-quality grind. Keep the patty simple; a nominal amount of spices and seasonings will really let the flavour of the beef come through. Try grating Vidalia onion right into the beef—its sweet, tangy taste blends right in.

To me, the ultimate condiment is a top-shelf barbecue sauce. My version has depth, spice, aroma, smoky flavour, and tang. Making it from scratch may be more effort than cracking a bottle of store-bought stuff, but after your first taste you'll never go back. It keeps really well, so make heaps at a time.

Topped with Cabbage-Celeriac Coleslaw, this burger is unbeatable. *{Serves 4}*

[TIMING IS EVERYTHING]

Prepare barbecue sauce and simmer (can be made up to 1 week in advance) •
Assemble patties (can be made up to 2 hours in advance) and refrigerate
• Make coleslaw (can be prepared up to 2 hours in advance and refrigerated) •
Prepare gravy for poutine • Grill burgers and keep warm • Finish poutine

MY WORLD FAMOUS BURGER

Patties

½ Vidalia onion, grated
2 Tbsp breadcrumbs
1 Tbsp Worcestershire sauce
1 Tbsp freshly ground black pepper
1½ tsp salt
1 tsp garlic powder
1½ lb ground sirloin

Burgers

4 hamburger buns
¼ cup olive oil
Homemade BBQ Sauce
Cabbage-Celeriac Coleslaw
  (see next page)
4 slices aged cheddar cheese

For the patties, in a large bowl, combine grated onion, breadcrumbs, Worcestershire sauce, black pepper, salt, garlic powder, and ground sirloin. Use your hands to combine well. Form into 4 patties and place on a baking sheet.

To finish the burgers, brush both sides of hamburger buns with olive oil. Spray grill rack with non-stick spray and preheat barbecue to medium-high heat. Grill burgers until lightly charred and cooked to desired doneness, about 6 to 8 minutes per side for medium-well. Grill buns, cut side down, about 2 minutes, or until golden.

To assemble burger, spread BBQ sauce on both sides of bun. Top with hamburger patty, coleslaw, and cheddar cheese. Serve with poutine.

HOMEMADE BBQ SAUCE

1 head garlic
1 large Vidalia onion, cut into
  large slices
1 Tbsp olive oil
salt and pepper
1 cup cider vinegar
3 bay leaves
½ cinnamon stick
1½ cups ketchup
¼ cup bourbon, plus a splash
  to finish sauce
2 Tbsp chopped chipotle peppers
  in adobo sauce
2 Tbsp molasses
2 Tbsp Worcestershire sauce
½ cup brown sugar
1 tsp ground cumin
1 tsp ground coriander
1 tsp freshly ground black pepper
1 tsp smoked paprika

Preheat oven to 400°F.

Slice ½ inch off the top of the garlic. Place Vidalia onion slices and head of garlic (cut side up) on separate pieces of aluminum foil. Drizzle each with olive oil and salt and pepper, and wrap tightly. Bake in preheated oven for 30 to 40 minutes, or until tender. Remove from oven, let cool, and squeeze out roasted garlic cloves. Discard skin. Maintain oven temperature.

Meanwhile, in a medium oven-proof saucepan, simmer cider vinegar with bay leaves and cinnamon stick until liquid has reduced by half, 7 to 8 minutes. Remove bay leaves and cinnamon.

Add ketchup, bourbon, chipotle peppers in sauce, molasses, and Worcestershire sauce to reduced cider vinegar. Stir to combine. Add brown sugar, cumin, coriander, pepper, and paprika. Stir to combine. Add reserved roasted garlic and onions. Purée with a hand-held immersion blender until smooth.

Transfer mixture to preheated oven and let sauce reduce 20 to 30 minutes, or until slightly charred around edges. Remove from oven; season with salt and pepper, and a splash of bourbon.

(continued on page 93 . . .)

91

(*continued from page 91*)

CABBAGE-CELERIAC COLESLAW

½ head celeriac, peeled
  and julienned
¼ head cabbage, core removed
  and julienned
1½ Tbsp kosher salt
½ small red onion, thinly sliced
¼ cup mayonnaise
2 Tbsp cider vinegar
1 Tbsp grainy mustard
1 tsp ground cumin
chopped cilantro, for garnish
salt and pepper

In a large bowl, toss celeriac and cabbage with salt. Let stand 10 to 15 minutes, then rinse and drain. In a small bowl, soak red onion in water for 10 minutes, then drain.

In a large bowl, toss celeriac, cabbage, and red onion together.

In a small bowl, combine mayonnaise, cider vinegar, grainy mustard, and cumin.

Add dressing to coleslaw and toss to combine. Garnish with fresh cilantro and season with salt and pepper.

POUTINE WITH HOMEMADE GRAVY AND DOUBLE-SMOKED BACON

French fries

4 large Yukon Gold potatoes,
  cut into ¾-inch strips
vegetable oil for frying
salt

Gravy

4 slices double-smoked bacon, diced
½ small onion, diced
¼ cup all-purpose flour
¼ cup white wine
1 tsp Worcestershire sauce
3 cups beef stock
freshly ground black pepper

Assembly

1 cup cheese curds
2 Tbsp chopped fresh thyme
coarse salt

For the french fries, place potatoes in a large pot. Fill with cold water, covering potatoes by 1 inch. Bring water up to a gentle simmer over medium heat and cook 3 to 5 minutes, or until tender. Drain potatoes and dry completely.

In a large, deep saucepan, heat oil to 375°F. Submerge half of the potatoes into oil and cook until golden brown, 4 to 5 minutes. Drain in paper towel–lined shallow dish and sprinkle with salt. Keep fries warm in a 200°F oven while frying the next batch.

For the gravy, sauté bacon in a medium saucepan for 8 to 10 minutes, or until golden and crispy. Remove bacon, leaving reserved bacon fat in pan. Add onion and sweat for 2 to 3 minutes, or until translucent. Add flour and whisk to combine, about 2 to 3 minutes. Add white wine and Worcestershire sauce to deglaze pan. Add stock and pepper and cook 3 to 4 minutes, or until gravy has thickened.

Remove fries from oven and increase the temperature to 400°F. To assemble poutine, divide fries among 4 small ovenproof dishes. Sprinkle with cheese curds and drizzle with gravy. Place in preheated oven until cheese starts to melt, about 2 minutes. Remove from oven and sprinkle with reserved bacon, fresh thyme, and coarse salt.

HONEY

Honey, known as liquid gold, is a naturally occurring sweetener made by honeybees. It's super-sweet and thick with a mild floral aroma and taste. Liquid honey comes in a variety of colours, from white to amber and from red to black. The general rule is that the darker the colour, the bolder the taste. The floral notes and consistency of honey vary a great deal depending on the flowers the honeybees are harvesting. While the most common varieties of honey are made from clover, alfalfa, and heather, there are also more fragrant varieties made from wildflowers or herbs like thyme and lavender.

SLOW-ROASTED PORK LOIN WITH
HONEY BALSAMIC GLAZE • **RUSTIC SAGE BREAD STUFFING** • GLAZED ROOT VEGETABLES • **APPLE ENDIVE SALAD WITH SWEET AND SPICY PECANS**

I grew up loving peanut butter, honey, and banana sandwiches. Another wonderful childhood food memory is a great Sunday night roast dinner. When you combine the two and add simple, hearty, and familiar ingredients, you're onto a seriously tasty main.

Pork and honey get along like peas and carrots. Adding balsamic vinegar to the pork's glaze gives it body, aroma, and depth, while Dijon mustard brings a little bite. The herbs are delicious with the pork and stuffing them directly into the flesh allows the flavour to permeate the meat as it cooks.

Honey's natural sweetness and the bright acidity of white wine turn humble root vegetables into a delicious side. The refreshing side salad's bitter endive and tart Granny Smith apple offsets the roasted vegetables' sweetness and warmth.

To me, the greatest home-cooked meals are often the simplest ones. Combining easy cooking techniques like roasting and glazing with the familiar sweetness and versatility of honey makes for a great way to eat. This meal reminds me of why I love simple comfort foods. Doing it up with the liquid gold? You bet that's a main! {Serves 4}

[TIMING IS EVERYTHING]

Prepare pecans for salad in advance • Glaze pork and roast • Prepare root vegetables and simmer • Assemble bread stuffing • Remove pork and prepare jus • Bake stuffing • Prepare salad • Carve pork loin at table

SLOW-ROASTED PORK LOIN WITH HONEY BALSAMIC GLAZE

one 4 lb pork loin roast, bone in
3–4 sprigs rosemary
3–4 sprigs thyme
salt and pepper
¼ cup balsamic vinegar
¼ cup white wine
¼ cup Dijon mustard
¼ cup honey
2 Tbsp olive oil
½ cup white wine
½ cup beef stock

Preheat oven to 350°F.

Score skin of pork roast. Cut along the bone, following bone down to the loin. Stuff pork with rosemary and thyme and season generously (both inside and out) with salt and pepper. With kitchen twine, tie roast in between each bone, securing tightly.

In a saucepan, combine balsamic vinegar, white wine, Dijon mustard, and honey. Stir over medium heat until mixture has reduced by half. Set aside.

In a large roasting pan, heat olive oil over medium-high heat. Add meat and sear on all sides until golden brown, about 8 to 10 minutes. Baste pork with reserved glaze.

Place roasting pan in preheated oven. Cook for 60 minutes, or until meat thermometer reaches 145°F, basting meat every 10 to 15 minutes. If pan appears dry, add extra water or wine, ½ cup at a time.

Remove from oven and deglaze pan with white wine and beef stock, making sure to scrape up all brown bits. Let rest for 10 minutes before serving. Reserve pan juices.

RUSTIC SAGE BREAD STUFFING

1 Tbsp olive oil
1 Tbsp butter
1–2 sprigs rosemary
1–2 sprigs sage
½ loaf country-style bread, torn into bite-sized pieces
salt and pepper
½ cup reserved pan juices from pork roast

Preheat oven to 350°F (oven should remain hot from pork roast).

In a medium sauté pan, heat oil, butter and fresh herbs until oil is fragrant, 1 to 2 minutes.

Add bread and season with salt and pepper. Put pan in preheated oven and bake for 10 minutes, or until bread is light golden.

Return pan to stovetop and add reserved pork pan drippings. Let liquid reduce slightly, then serve immediately.

GLAZED ROOT VEGETABLES

1 Tbsp olive oil
1 medium parsnip, peeled and cut into 2-inch pieces
½ medium turnip, peeled and cut into 2-inch pieces
1 large carrot, peeled and cut into 2-inch pieces
1 leek, cleaned, cut into ½-inch rounds
2 cups Brussels sprouts, sliced in half
1 Tbsp butter
1–2 sprigs thyme
¼ cup white wine
1 Tbsp honey
salt and pepper

In a medium sauté pan, heat oil over medium heat. Add parsnip, turnip, and carrot, and sauté 2 to 3 minutes, or until lightly browned. Add leek, Brussels sprouts, and butter. When butter starts to foam, add thyme and sauté for another 2 to 3 minutes, or until vegetables are lightly browned.

Add white wine, honey, and salt and pepper. Cover pan and simmer over medium heat for 10 to 15 minutes, or until vegetables are tender.

APPLE ENDIVE SALAD WITH SWEET AND SPICY PECANS

¼ cup honey
½ tsp cayenne
1 cup whole pecans
3 heads Belgian endive, julienned
1 Granny Smith apple
juice of ½ lemon
2 Tbsp olive oil
salt and pepper

Preheat oven to 400°F.

In a medium bowl, combine honey and cayenne. Add nuts and toss until evenly coated with honey mixture. Spread mixture onto a parchment-lined baking sheet and bake in preheated oven for 10 to 12 minutes, or until nuts are toasted. Let cool and chop coarsely.

In a large bowl, toss together endive, apple, and honey-spiced pecans. Add lemon juice, olive oil, and salt and pepper. Toss to combine.

JERK SPICE

Jerk is a traditional Jamaican spice mix, but its exact origins are unknown. Allspice, Scotch bonnet peppers (one of the hottest), and salt are at the heart of jerk spice, but other ingredients can be added to make varying blends—try scallions, garlic, thyme, cinnamon, and nutmeg. Jerk

rubs and marinades vary a great deal, not just regionally but even from family to family. The recipes, often closely guarded family secrets, are passed from one generation to the next.

Jerk spices are combined to make a dry rub that is worked into meat before cooking, or blended

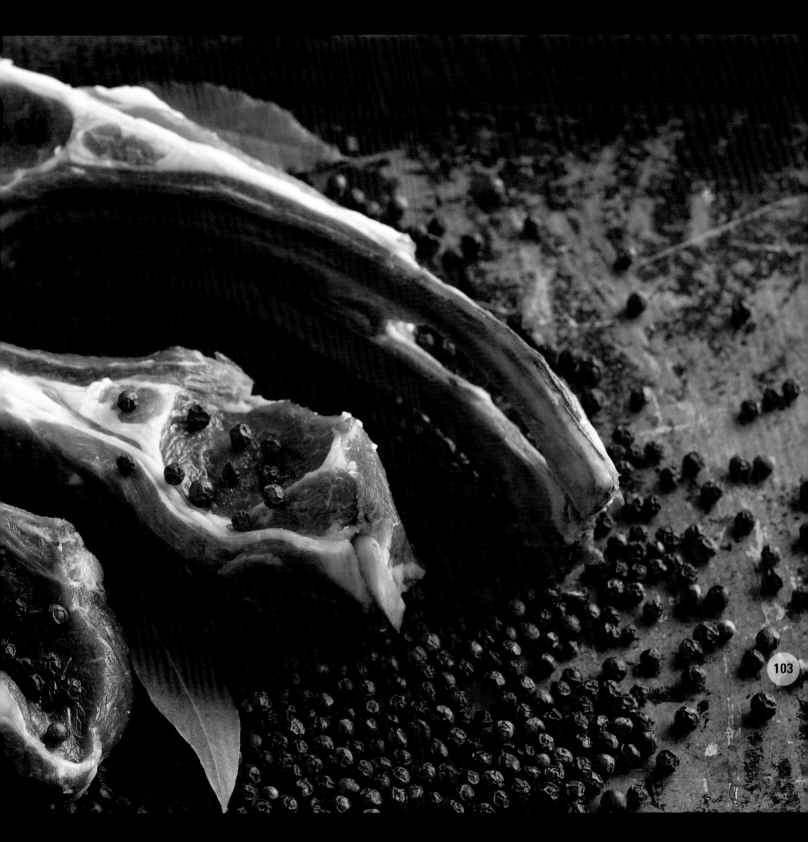

rack between medium-rare and medium; cooked
any less it will be chewy, and cooked any more it
will become tough.

GRILLED LAMB CHOPS WITH FRESH HERBS, LEMON, AND GARLIC · SUMMER SALAD · MINTED COUSCOUS WITH TOASTED ALMONDS · TZATZIKI

I n the spirit of true Mediterranean cuisine, this main has a great balance of flavours, textures, aromas, and colours. It is inspired by my travels through Greece, where the food is a cornucopia of vibrant flavours. The lamb dishes in Greece are incredible and I have recreated the taste here by doing the meat up with a delicious combination of garlic, rosemary, and mustard. The fluffy, minted couscous is true to the Greek theme and I love how it soaks up all the juice from the lamb.

All these delicious Greek-inspired dishes wouldn't be the same without the tzatziki. Thick, creamy, and cool, this tzatziki incorporates the usual suspects—sharp, raw garlic and cool cucumber. I've taken it to the next level and added mint to make it even more refreshing. By straining the already thick Greek yogurt, you'll get a thick, super-creamy tzatziki. {Serves 4}

[TIMING IS EVERYTHING]
Prepare tzatziki (can be made up to 2 days in advance and refrigerated) •
Marinate lamb • Steep couscous • Toast almonds • Finish couscous • Prepare
salad • Grill lamb to medium-rare

GRILLED LAMB CHOPS WITH FRESH HERBS, LEMON, AND GARLIC

Lamb marinade

3 medium cloves garlic, minced
3 Tbsp fresh rosemary, chopped
⅓ cup chopped parsley
2 Tbsp Dijon mustard
⅓ cup olive oil
½ tsp pepper

Lamb

2 racks of lamb, each cut into 6 chops
coarse sea salt
1 lemon, squeezed for juice

For the marinade, in a medium mixing bowl, combine garlic, rosemary, parsley, Dijon mustard, olive oil, and pepper, and smear all over lamb chops. Place on a plate, cover, and marinate for at least 60 minutes in the refrigerator.

Just before grilling, season lamb generously with coarse sea salt. Grill on high heat 2 to 3 minutes on each side, including fat side. Squeeze lemon juice over chops while cooking. Remove from heat and let rest.

SUMMER SALAD

1 bunch asparagus, stringy
   ends peeled
2 medium zucchini, cut lengthwise
   into ¼-inch strips
½ pint grape tomatoes, halved
½ red onion, sliced very thinly and
   soaked in cold water
2 Tbsp olive oil
salt

Bring a large pot of salted water to a rolling boil. Cut asparagus into 1½-inch lengths. Add asparagus to boiling water; cook until spears are still crisp, about 1 minute. Add zucchini and cook for only 1 minute. Strain asparagus and zucchini; plunge immediately into ice water or rinse under cold running water. Transfer to a medium mixing bowl; add tomatoes, sliced red onion, olive oil, and salt. Set aside.

MINTED COUSCOUS WITH TOASTED ALMONDS

1 cup couscous
1 cup water
¼ cup chopped mint
3 Tbsp flaked almonds, toasted
juice and zest of ½ lemon
2 Tbsp olive oil
salt and pepper

Bring water to a boil. Pour boiling water over couscous; cover and let stand 5 minutes. Fluff with a fork and stir in mint, almonds, lemon juice and zest, olive oil, and salt and pepper.

TZATZIKI

2 cups Greek (or whole-milk)
   yogurt, drained
½ English cucumber, peeled
   and grated
pinch of salt
1 small clove garlic, finely minced
handful chopped fresh mint
coarse salt
freshly ground black pepper

Hang yogurt in a sieve or fine mesh strainer over a medium bowl. Let stand at least 60 minutes, letting excess liquid drain away. Very lightly salt grated cucumber and drain in same way for 20 to 30 minutes.

Combine drained yogurt, grated cucumber, garlic, and mint in a medium bowl. Season with coarse salt and freshly ground black pepper. Keep refrigerated.

105

LENTILS

Once thought of as "poor man's meat," lentils are a healthy, hearty legume that forms the basis of a lot of great dishes. There are many varieties out there: black, green, yellow, orange, red, beluga, and du Puy, to name a few. Try them all, but keep in mind that the yellow, orange, and red varieties fall apart choice for soups and stews. If you're after a lentil that holds its shape, go for the darker varieties. Remember that lentils—like rice, pasta, or grains— are a great base, but usually need the help of other big flavours to really kick things off. Try them with cured meats: chorizo, Italian sausage, pancetta,

If you know you're going to be cooking with lentils, try soaking them in cold water in the fridge overnight. This cuts the cooking time in half and allows them to hold their beautiful shape while cooking evenly. And be sure to give them a good rinse beforehand in cold water; lentils often get shipped in large canvas sacks and need a thorough cleaning. Finally, lentils can be stored for five to six months in an airtight container, making them perfect for when you're wondering: "What's for dinner?"

SLOW-BRAISED LENTILS WITH DOUBLE-SMOKED BACON, WHITE WINE, AND CRÈME FRAÎCHE · THYME AND DIJON MUSTARD CRUSTED PORK CHOPS · WARM APPLE COMPOTE WITH CALVADOS AND GOLDEN RAISINS

I've always said that an average cook can make a good meal out of top-notch ingredients, but an amazing cook can make a spectacular meal with the most humble ingredients. This main is about making simple ingredients into something remarkable.

When I was working as the sous-chef at La Trompette, a high-end restaurant in London, England, we cooked a roast every Sunday and it was a very popular event. One Sunday, the executive chef was away and all the responsibilities fell to me. It was busy, but I came up with this amazing roast. Here, I've adjusted it to individual chops to fit in the average household oven.

I've built this main around lentils because they soak up flavour so well. They are essentially twice cooked here—first to reconstitute and soften them and then again to braise them and infuse them with flavour. They pick up the aromas of the double-smoked bacon, carrot, onion, leek, white wine, stock, and crème fraîche.

This dish is crowned with apple compote, which features raisins and Calvados—a dry apple brandy. Apples pair nicely with pork chops and this jam-like sauce really rounds out the main beautifully. {Serves 4}

[TIMING IS EVERYTHING]

Pre-cook lentils • Prepare compote and set aside • Braise lentils and roast pork chops • Set chops aside to rest and finish lentils • Divide lentils onto 4 plates • Top with pork chops and drizzle with any pan juices • Serve with compote

SLOW-BRAISED LENTILS WITH DOUBLE-SMOKED BACON, WHITE WINE, AND CRÈME FRAÎCHE

Pre-cooking

1 cup dried lentils, rinsed and
  drained

½ small onion

1 small stalk celery, whole

1 small carrot, cut lengthwise

2 bay leaves

salt and pepper

For braising lentils

1 tsp vegetable oil

4 slices double-smoked bacon, diced

¼ cup finely diced carrot

⅓ cup finely diced onion

⅓ cup finely diced leek

1 clove garlic, finely minced

¼ cup white wine

1 cup chicken stock

3 Tbsp butter

2 Tbsp crème fraîche

¼ cup chopped parsley

salt and pepper

Combine lentils, onion, celery, carrot, and bay leaves in a medium saucepan. Cover with cold water to about 1 inch above lentils. Simmer uncovered until lentils are cooked and liquid has mostly evaporated, about 20 to 25 minutes. Season with salt and pepper.

Heat vegetable oil in a large, wide skillet over medium-high heat. Add bacon pieces and cook until slightly crispy. Add carrot, onion, leek, and garlic, and gently sweat for a few minutes. Add white wine to deglaze, making sure to scrape up any crispy brown bits. Add chicken stock and pre-cooked lentils; bring to a simmer and reduce until liquid reaches a light sauce consistency. To finish, gently stir in butter, crème fraîche, and parsley. Season with salt and pepper.

THYME AND DIJON MUSTARD CRUSTED PORK CHOPS

3–4 sprigs thyme

2 Tbsp Dijon mustard

coarse salt and pepper

4 pork chops

2 Tbsp vegetable oil

Preheat oven to 350°F.

Pick off and roughly chop thyme leaves. Smear a good amount of Dijon mustard on chops and season well with chopped thyme and salt and pepper. Heat vegetable oil in a large, wide ovenproof pan over medium heat.

Carefully place chops in pan and sear each side until browned, about 1 minute. Place pan in oven on middle rack for 5 to 6 minutes; test for doneness and rest for at least 5 minutes before serving.

WARM APPLE COMPOTE WITH CALVADOS AND GOLDEN RAISINS

¼ cup Calvados

¼ cup golden raisins

2 Tbsp butter

2 Fuji (or Matsu) apples, peeled,
  cored, and diced

pinch of brown sugar

salt and pepper

Gently heat Calvados and raisins in a small saucepan. Heat butter in a large skillet over medium-high heat. Add apples and brown sugar; sauté until light golden, about 3 minutes. Take skillet off heat, add Calvados, and return to heat. If desired, light pan and let alcohol burn off. Otherwise, let liquid simmer, reducing slightly. Season with salt and pepper.

L O B S T E R

Bigger is not necessarily always better: it isn't the size of your lobster that matters but how you cook it. In fact, the older and larger the lobster, the tougher its meat will be when cooked. Young lobsters are more tender, but offer less meat relative to shell. For the best bang for your buck, look for lobsters that are about one-and-a-half pounds.

Lobster is often sold live because it should be as fresh as possible. When you're purchasing lobster, make sure it's in a large clean tank of salt water, and that it's moving and frisky when handled. If you can touch a lobster with no noticeable reaction, chances are that it's on its last legs and not worth your money. For optimum freshness, buy live

lobster the same day you intend to cook it.

When it comes to cooking lobster, there are two major schools of thought: steaming and boiling. I prefer to boil my lobster as I find steaming can actually dry it out. A one-and-a-half-pound lobster takes about seven to eight minutes in rolling boiling water. Once it's done, place it into an ice bath (ice and water) for a few minutes to stop it from overcooking.

ROAST LOBSTER WITH CHORIZO AND HOT SMOKED PAPRIKA · **WHIPPED POTATOES** · SWEET CORN AND BASIL · **CHARRED SCALLION AND GARLIC BUTTER**

This main makes cooking lobster, an ingredient a lot of people find daunting, a breeze. It also features some great flavour combinations. The fresh lobster's meaty texture and natural sweetness lends itself nicely to the smoky chorizo and the hot smoked paprika (if you're not feeling up to the heat, you can substitute with sweet smoked paprika). The Sweet Corn and Basil is a great accompaniment to this dish—the corn and crisp white wine keep things fresh, while the basil brings a fragrant cooling effect.

I've topped this main with Charred Scallion and Garlic Butter. I've always been a huge fan of flavoured butters. Sometimes known as compound butters, they're dead easy to whip up and freeze exceptionally well, making them the perfect make-ahead alternative to a sauce. I don't think I need to explain the combination of garlic, butter, and lobster—it is straight-up perfection!

I love this dish on a summer evening with a good glass of white wine. It's also the perfect meal to eat out at the cabin while you watch the sun set. {Serves 4}

[TIMING IS EVERYTHING]

Boil potatoes • Prepare Sweet Corn and Basil • Prepare butter (can also be prepared up to 1 month in advance and frozen) • Whip potatoes • Assemble and cook lobster • Divide potatoes onto 4 plates • Top with lobster tails and claws, chorizo-parsley mixture, and Sweet Corn and Basil • Garnish with paprika

ROAST LOBSTER WITH CHORIZO AND HOT SMOKED PAPRIKA

four 1½ lb lobsters
3 Tbsp butter
1 Tbsp olive oil
1 clove garlic, roughly chopped
½ cup diced chorizo
1 tsp hot smoked paprika
juice of ½ lemon
2 Tbsp chopped parsley

To blanch lobsters, bring a large pot of salted water to a rolling boil. Add lobsters and cook for about 7 to 8 minutes. Remove from pot. When cool enough to handle, separate tail from body. Cut tail in half lengthwise. Pick out claw and leg meat, keeping pieces as whole as possible.

Preheat oven to 350°F.

Place butter, olive oil, and garlic in a large, cold cast iron or heavy-bottomed pan and bring up to medium heat. Just as garlic starts to lightly colour, add diced chorizo.

Season lobster tails and claw meat with paprika. Add lobster meat to pan, placing tails flesh side down. Finish cooking in the preheated oven for about 4 minutes. Remove and add lemon juice and parsley.

WHIPPED POTATOES

2 lb Yukon Gold potatoes (about 5 medium), peeled and quartered
1 bay leaf
¼ cup whipping cream (35%)
½ lb butter, cubed and at room temperature
salt and pepper

Put potatoes and bay leaf in a medium pot. Fill pot with cold water just to cover potatoes; season cooking water well with salt (it should taste like the sea) and bring to a boil. Boil on medium-high heat until potatoes are tender but not overdone, about 10 to 15 minutes. Strain potatoes; let dry out slightly in colander before returning to pot. Add whipping cream, butter, pepper, and more salt if necessary. Whip with electric beaters just to combine. (Do not overmix or potatoes will become gummy.) Keep warm.

SWEET CORN AND BASIL

4 cups corn kernels, fresh or frozen
1 Tbsp butter
1 Tbsp olive oil
½ onion, finely diced
2 Tbsp white wine
2 Tbsp chopped basil
salt and pepper

Bring a large pot of salted water to a rolling boil. Add corn and cook for 1 minute; drain. Heat butter and olive oil in a pan over medium heat. Add onion and sweat until slightly softened, about 2 minutes. Add corn and white wine; cover and simmer until tender, about 4 to 5 minutes. Remove from heat and stir in basil; season with salt and pepper.

CHARRED SCALLION AND GARLIC BUTTER

½ lb butter
4 scallions
2 cloves garlic, chopped

Preheat barbecue or indoor grill to high heat.

Melt butter in a small saucepan. Meanwhile, grill scallions until softened and charred. Let cool slightly and roughly chop. Add scallions and garlic to melted butter. Let stand in a warm place to allow flavours to infuse.

113

MAPLE SYRUP

A quintessentially Canadian ingredient, maple syrup has a beautiful depth and distinction and a fragrant vanilla aroma. It has a clear, amber colour and a thick consistency, which is achieved by simmering the sap of the maple tree for hours. It takes between 30 and 40 litres of maple sap to make a single litre of maple syrup. First

Nations people have been making maple syrup for years, and early European settlers adopted their techniques. February, March, and April are the primary production months.

Maple syrup is great in or on just about anything. There's the obvious: pancakes (short stacks and tall stacks alike), flapjacks, waffles

MAPLE-GLAZED SALMON
FILLETS WITH SEARED ROSEMARY · BACON
BARLEY · SAUTÉED SWISS
CHARD · MAPLE BACON

This marinade works well with other rich fish like black cod (sablefish) or sea bass, but I like to use salmon because its rich buttery texture is perfect with the sweet syrup, and it brings the dish back to its First Nations roots. Cooking the salmon in a hot cast iron skillet helps to develop good colour and to caramelize the maple syrup as the fish sears. When purchasing salmon, look for clean-smelling fish with firm, tight flesh.

My Bacon Barley provides this main with a great base. I love barley as a side because it's both simple to prepare and hearty. The onions and garlic bring a savoury flavour while the salty bacon works well with the sweetness of the maple marinade.

Swiss chard is a tasty and hearty green. It does have a slight bitterness, but it is offset in this main by the sweetness of the corn. The acidity of the white wine keeps this dish light and the chicken stock gives it body. It's all very healthy, so you can feel great about eating it! {Serves 4}

Marinate fish • Prepare and cook Maple Bacon • Prepare Bacon Barley and Swiss chard • Sear fish • Place small mound of Bacon Barley on a plate and top with Swiss chard • Place 3 pieces of salmon on top • Garnish with Maple Bacon

MAPLE-GLAZED SALMON FILLETS WITH SEARED ROSEMARY

½ cup maple syrup

¼ cup soy sauce

1 Tbsp cider vinegar

1 Tbsp freshly ground black pepper

1 rosemary sprig, crushed to release oils

four 6 oz salmon fillets, each sliced lengthwise into 3 strips

1 Tbsp vegetable oil

In a small ceramic dish large enough to hold the salmon, combine maple syrup, soy sauce, cider vinegar, black pepper, and rosemary sprig. Add salmon and let marinate for 2 hours in the refrigerator.

In a medium cast iron skillet, heat vegetable oil over medium-high heat. Add salmon and cook 20 to 30 seconds per side, or until fish is cooked to medium doneness.

BACON BARLEY

1 Tbsp olive oil

4 strips bacon, chopped

1 small onion, diced

1 clove garlic, minced

1 sprig rosemary, leaves only

1 cup white wine

2 cups cooked barley, cooked according to package directions

In a large skillet, heat olive oil over medium heat. Add bacon and cook 4 to 6 minutes, or until golden brown and crispy. Add onion and cook 5 more minutes, or until soft and translucent. Add garlic and rosemary leaves. Stir to combine.

Add white wine to deglaze pan. Add barley and stir to combine.

SAUTÉED SWISS CHARD

1 bunch Swiss chard

1 Tbsp olive oil

1 cup corn, fresh or frozen

2 Tbsp white wine or chicken stock

Clean Swiss chard and remove stems. Cut stems into 1-inch pieces and tear greens into bite-sized pieces. Keep stems and greens separate.

In a large skillet, heat olive oil over medium heat. Add Swiss chard stems and corn and cook 3 to 4 minutes, or until tender. Add white wine or stock and let liquid reduce slightly, another 3 to 4 minutes. Add greens and cook 2 to 3 minutes, or until wilted.

MAPLE BACON

4 strips bacon

⅓ cup maple syrup

Preheat oven to 400°F.

Place bacon on a baking sheet and put into oven. Bake for 10 minutes.

Brush maple syrup onto bacon and return to oven. Baste bacon with maple syrup every 5 to 10 minutes, or until bacon is golden and crispy, for a total of 25 to 30 minutes. Let cool and break into pieces.

MEDITERRANEAN HERBS

Thyme, oregano, marjoram, and basil are absolutely essential elements of the Mediterranean's unique cuisine. (Other Mediterranean herbs include rosemary, sage, savory, tarragon, and bay leaf, with parsley being the most common.) Using these herbs appropriately in simple dishes can really take your food to the next level and help you achieve a truly authentic taste.

THYME is the most widely used Mediterranean herb and there are over 350 different kinds. It's fragrant and flavourful without being overpowering, making it easy to pair with other herbs and spices.

OREGANO is absolutely indispensable to Greek and Italian cuisine. (In fact, it deserves its own

section—see page 126.) It's intensely aromatic and comes in many varieties, which range in taste from warm and slightly bitter to peppery.

MARJORAM is slightly less common, but still a key Mediterranean herb. It features aromatic leaves with a citrus and sweet pine flavour.

BASIL is a staple in sweet and savoury dishes, and an incredibly versatile herb. Italian basil is the most common strain; its broad, tender leaves have a pungent, sweetly floral aroma and mild anise flavour. (For more on basil, see page 16).

MEDITERRANEAN SHAVED
VEAL · LEMON POTATO PURÉE · RED PEPPER
BALSAMIC JAM WITH BASIL

Using Mediterranean herbs is a great way to elevate your cooking and bring an authentic taste to a rustic home-cooked meal. I've always said that thyme would be my desert island herb because its warm, aromatic fragrance and simple taste go with almost anything. Veal is another important ingredient in Mediterranean cuisine, so combining it with the herbs makes for a deliciously authentic dish. There are a few different varieties of veal and they all have a delicate flavour that lends well to pairing. Veal is also fairly lean, making it one of the healthier red meats.

My Mediterranean Shaved Veal is complemented perfectly by my Lemon Potato Purée, which includes the rich tang of sour cream and the fruity taste and velvety texture of olive oil. A serving of tangy Red Pepper Balsamic Jam with Basil rounds out this main. I love it because it's outstanding with both meat and fish, and it can also be used as a condiment or topping. {Serves 4}

RED PEPPER BALSAMIC JAM WITH BASIL

4 red peppers
2 Tbsp olive oil
¼ cup finely diced red onion
1 clove garlic, finely diced
salt and pepper
1½ Tbsp balsamic vinegar
1 Tbsp chopped basil

Char peppers on a barbecue grill or broil in oven for 10 to 15 minutes, or until blackened on all sides. Transfer peppers to a large bowl and cover with plastic wrap. Let stand 15 minutes. Peel, seed, and dice peppers.

In a medium skillet, heat olive oil over medium heat. Add onion and cook 4 to 5 minutes, or until soft and translucent. Add garlic and cook another 2 to 3 minutes. Add diced roasted red peppers and cook 2 to 3 minutes more, or until vegetables are soft. Season with salt and pepper. Add balsamic vinegar and let liquid reduce on low heat for 5 minutes. Remove from heat and let cool.

Add basil and stir to combine.

MEDITERRANEAN SHAVED VEAL

one 2 lb veal eye round roast, trimmed of sinew
salt and pepper
2 Tbsp olive oil
¼ cup coarsely chopped fresh Mediterranean herbs (such as thyme, marjoram, oregano), stems reserved
2 cloves garlic, finely chopped
zest of ½ lemon
juice of ½ lemon
¼ cup white wine

Preheat oven to 350°F. Season veal roast with salt and pepper.

In a large skillet, heat olive oil over medium-high heat. Add veal and sear on all sides, 8 to 10 minutes in total, or until golden. Transfer veal to a roasting pan.

In a small bowl, combine Mediterranean herbs, garlic, and lemon zest. Rub mixture all over seared veal.

Place roasting pan in preheated oven and cook for 30 to 40 minutes, or until cooked through. Halfway through cooking, squeeze lemon juice on top of veal.

Remove from oven and add white wine to deglaze the pan, scraping up all brown bits.

Let meat rest for 5 minutes. Slice meat very thinly and return slices to roasting pan to let all the juices absorb.

LEMON POTATO PURÉE

6 medium-sized white potatoes, peeled and cut into quarters
½ cup milk
½ cup sour cream
2 Tbsp olive oil
zest of 1 lemon
salt and pepper

Place potatoes in a large pot of cold salted water. Bring to a boil and cook until potatoes are fork tender, 15 to 20 minutes. Drain potatoes.

In a medium saucepan, heat milk over medium heat. Add sour cream, olive oil, and lemon zest.

Transfer potatoes to bowl of a stand mixer. Add milk mixture and beat at high speed with whisk attachment for 10 to 20 seconds (you can also use a hand mixer), or until smooth. Do not overmix. Season with salt and pepper.

121

ONIONS

There aren't many savoury recipes that don't start out with an onion. I've grown to love the humble and reliable onion, not just to get a great recipe kicked off, but also front and centre at the heart of an incredible main. As a young chef, I was astonished by the amount of different varieties

there are—green onions, shallots, white, yellow, and purple onions, and, of course, my all-time favourite: Vidalia onions.

If you've never had the pleasure of enjoying one of these gems, get your hands on one now. Vidalia onions are visually similar to broad yellow onions

and often have torn papery skin. Inside, they have
large thick layers that are perfect for onion rings.
The Vidalia's most remarkable feature, though,

TENDERLOIN STEAK SANDWICH WITH STICKY CARAMELIZED ONIONS, SAUTÉED MUSHROOMS, AND ARUGULA · CRISPY BUTTERMILK ONION RINGS · DOUBLE-ONION DIP

I love a good steak sandwich, and the best ones I've had are at home or at friends' houses, not at restaurants. I think the first thing restaurants get wrong is that they often use cheaper, tougher cuts of steak, and you'd be hard pressed to bite through one without the entire steak sliding out from between the two pieces of bread. Some restaurants do use nicer cuts like strip or rib eye, but often fail to slice them up properly, and the results are usually messy.

The solution is a beautifully cooked piece of mustard-crusted beef tenderloin that's been prop-

erly rested and thinly sliced. It's melt-in-your-mouth meat, perfect for working into a killer sandwich with caramelized onions, sautéed buttered mushrooms, and peppery arugula all on a toasty baguette.

My buttermilk onion rings set the bar high. Sweet Vidalia onions are incredible to begin with, and after a nice soak in some tangy buttermilk, then getting battered and fried up, they are amazing.

This main is a great example of the flavour and versatility of the modest onion. {Serves 4}

[TIMING IS EVERYTHING]

Soak onion rings in buttermilk • Roast onions for dip • Sear steak and prepare onions and mushrooms for sandwich; keep warm • Finish dip • Fry onion rings • Assemble sandwiches

TENDERLOIN STEAK SANDWICH WITH STICKY CARAMELIZED ONIONS, SAUTÉED MUSHROOMS, AND ARUGULA

Steak

1 Tbsp Dijon mustard
1 Tbsp whole grain mustard
one 8–10 oz portion beef tenderloin
2 Tbsp coarse sea salt
2 Tbsp coarsely cracked black pepper
3 Tbsp olive oil

Onions and mushrooms

4 Tbsp butter (divided)
4 Tbsp olive oil (divided)
2 onions, thinly sliced
4 cups mixed mushrooms (cremini, portobello, and button are ideal)
1 sprig thyme
salt and pepper

Sandwich

1 Tbsp Dijon mustard
1 Tbsp whole grain mustard
1 French baguette
1 cup baby arugula, washed

Preheat oven to 400°F.

To prepare steak, combine Dijon and whole grain mustards in a small bowl. Smear beef tenderloin with mustard mixture and then coat with sea salt and pepper on all sides to form a crust. Heat olive oil in a cast iron or heavy ovenproof skillet over high heat. When oil begins to smoke, sear all sides of beef until crust is deep golden brown. Place skillet in oven to finish cooking, about 10 minutes for medium-rare. Remove from heat and let rest at least 15 minutes.

To prepare onions, heat 2 Tbsp butter and 2 Tbsp olive oil in a medium skillet over medium heat. Sauté onions until softened and lightly coloured, about 5 to 7 minutes. Season with salt and pepper and set aside. To prepare mushrooms, heat remaining 2 Tbsp butter and 2 Tbsp olive oil in a medium skillet over high heat. Sauté mushrooms and thyme until well coloured, about 8 to 10 minutes. Season with salt and pepper.

To assemble sandwiches, combine Dijon and whole grain mustards. Carve steak into thin slices, reserving any juices. Split baguette into 4 portions. Toast each lightly and spread thinly with mustard mixture. Fill each sandwich with steak, sautéed onions, and mushrooms. Top with arugula and spoon over any steak juices. Serve with hot onion rings.

CRISPY BUTTERMILK ONION RINGS

3 cups buttermilk
1 Tbsp garlic powder
1 sprig thyme, leaves only
1 sprig marjoram, leaves only
1 Tbsp salt
1 tsp pepper
2 Vidalia onions, cut into ½-inch-thick rings
2¼ cups flour (divided)
4 cups vegetable oil for frying

Combine buttermilk, garlic powder, thyme leaves, marjoram leaves, and salt and pepper in a large bowl. Soak onion slices, making sure they are covered in buttermilk mixture, in the refrigerator for at least 60 minutes; overnight is best.

Preheat oven to 250°F.

Drain onions, reserving buttermilk marinade. Place 2 cups of the flour in a medium mixing bowl; slowly whisk in enough reserved marinade (about 2 cups) to form a loose paste the consistency of pancake batter.

Fill a small deep saucepan about 1½ to 2 inches deep with vegetable oil, making sure oil does not reach more than halfway up saucepan. Heat oil to 340–350°F. Lightly flour onion rings with remaining ¼ cup flour. Dip into batter and drop, 1 or 2 at a time, into oil. Fry until deep golden brown and drain on a paper towel–lined plate. Season onion rings with salt while still warm. Keep onion rings warm.

DOUBLE-ONION DIP

1 cup roughly chopped Vidalia onions (leftover pieces from the onion ring recipe can be used)
1 Tbsp olive oil
¾ cup sour cream
¾ cup mayonnaise
2–3 dashes hot sauce
2 green onions, chopped
salt

Preheat oven to 350°F.

Place Vidalia onions in a piece of aluminum foil and drizzle olive oil over them. Wrap in a loose package and bake until tender and golden, about 15 to 20 minutes. Unwrap and when cool enough to handle, chop into a rough mash. Combine sour cream, mayonnaise, and hot sauce in a medium bowl. Add chopped onion and green onions. Fold to combine and season with salt. Cover with plastic wrap and keep refrigerated.

OREGANO

Oregano is an intensely aromatic herb that can range in taste from warm and slightly bitter to peppery. It is sometimes mistakenly referred to as "wild marjoram" because the two herbs taste similar.

Oregano, which translates to "joy of the moun-

part of Italian and Greek cuisine. It is often used alongside sweet basil in sauces, on roasted meats, and, of course, on pizza. In fact, another one of oregano's nicknames is the "pizza herb."

When you're buying fresh oregano, look for vibrant green colour without any yellowish tinges.

OREGANO-CRUSTED LEG OF LAMB WITH GARLIC · ROASTED LEMON POTATOES WITH OREGANO · GREEK SALAD WITH RED WINE AND FETA VINAIGRETTE · GRILLED PITA

I love going out for Greek food, and I've pulled out all the stops with this main to help you bring some of the best restaurant-style Greek food you can imagine into your kitchen. Oregano is the key to making authentic Greek food, and this main puts the herb front and centre.

A leg of lamb makes for some pretty serious eating. Encrusted with garlic and oregano, this lamb dish is rustic, delicious, and large—perfect for enjoying with friends.

I find when I go out for top-notch Greek, my friends just can't get enough of the roasted potatoes. This version is the real deal: effortless and incredible.

No Greek meal is complete without a delicious Greek salad. Since you can't really waver on the ingredients of a classic Greek salad, the dressing is key, and this one sets the bar high. It's delicious and keeps well, so I suggest making extra. In fact, you'll end up using it to dress all sorts of salads. {Serves 4}

OREGANO-CRUSTED LEG OF LAMB WITH GARLIC

2 bunches oregano, leaves picked
  and roughly chopped
4 cloves of garlic, peeled and
  chopped
zest of ½ lemon
¼ cup olive oil
salt and pepper
1 small (4–4.5 lb) boneless
  leg of lamb

Preheat oven to 375°F.

Combine oregano, garlic, lemon zest, and olive oil in a small mixing bowl. Season lamb generously with salt and pepper. Rub inside and outside of lamb with marinade. Roll leg back up and truss with butcher string.

Preheat barbecue or indoor grill to medium-high heat.

Pat any excess olive oil off lamb leg. Grill lamb leg until all sides have developed a rich, deep brown crust. Place lamb into a roasting pan and roast in the oven, basting occasionally with pan juices, about 1½ hours, or until thermometer inserted in thickest part of leg registers 150°F. Allow lamb to rest, covered, for at least 10 minutes.

ROASTED LEMON POTATOES WITH OREGANO

3 Tbsp olive oil
15–18 small new potatoes
  (about ¾ lb)
1 tsp dried oregano
salt and pepper
1 Tbsp butter
juice of 1 lemon

Preheat oven to 350°F.

Heat olive oil in a large, ovenproof skillet over high heat. Add potatoes, searing until sides are golden brown. Season with oregano and salt and pepper. Add butter and place pan into oven. Bake until potatoes are tender, about 30 minutes. Remove from heat, add lemon juice, and season with additional salt and pepper.

GREEK SALAD WITH RED WINE AND FETA VINAIGRETTE

Salad

2 medium ripe tomatoes, cored and
  cut into bite-sized wedges
1 red pepper, cored, seeds removed,
  cut into bite-sized pieces
1 cucumber, peeled and cut into
  bite-sized pieces
1 red onion, cut into bite-sized
  pieces, soaked in cold water and
  drained
¼ cup black olives, pitted
1 cup feta, cut into 1-inch cubes
1 Tbsp fresh oregano

Dressing

1 Tbsp feta cheese, finely crumbled
1 tsp dried oregano
1 small clove garlic, finely minced
juice and zest of 1 lemon
2 Tbsp red wine vinegar
2 Tbsp olive oil
salt and pepper

To prepare dressing, whisk together all ingredients and season with salt and pepper. Combine salad ingredients and dressing in a large mixing bowl and toss to combine.

GRILLED PITA

4–5 pitas
1 Tbsp olive oil

Preheat barbecue or indoor grill to medium-high heat. Lightly brush olive oil on both sides of pitas; grill until golden and warmed through.

OYSTERS

Lovers have held oysters in high esteem for centuries—the shellfish is infamous as a powerful aphrodisiac. Casanova, the king of lovers, reportedly used to knock back a dozen before every dinner, and Roman emperors bought them for their weight in gold. Aphrodisiac powers aside, oysters are a popular delicacy prized for

their nutty flavour and briny tang. A classic way to serve them is chilled with a mignonette—a simple and delicious combination of red wine, red wine vinegar, shallots, and freshly ground pepper.

There are many varieties of oysters, ranging in texture, size, and taste. Tasting them is similar to enjoying fine wines; they can be light or full-bodied

CLASSIC OYSTERS ROCKEFELLER · **OYSTERS STRAIGHT-UP WITH MIGNONETTE** · HOMEMADE FRITES · **LEMON ROSEMARY MAYONNAISE**

Oysters Rockefeller is probably the most famous oyster dish in North America. It was invented in 1899 by the owner of Antoine's restaurant in New Orleans and named after John D. Rockefeller. My own version combines oysters with crispy bacon, savoury shallots, a fresh hint of white wine, and Pernod—a licorice-flavoured liqueur that pairs well with oysters. Baking and serving Oysters Rockefeller on salt keeps them from tipping over.

The best side with oysters is undoubtedly frites, which are like french fries but about the width of matchsticks. Russet potatoes make the best frites because their starch holds them together and their high sugar content makes them fry up golden brown and crispy. Frites need a great dip, and mine is easy and delicious; mayonnaise provides a creamy base, lemon juice adds acidity, and rosemary brings a tasty twist.

Whether you do them up with this famous American recipe or serve them simply, oysters really are the perfect food. I'll always remember my first oyster. I was very young and my chef pressured me into eating one. I was nervous but I closed my eyes and knocked it back. I've loved them ever since! *{Serves 4}*

[TIMING IS EVERYTHING]

Cut and soak potatoes for frites • Prepare mignonette and mayonnaise (can both be made in advance and refrigerated—mignonette for up to 1 month and mayonnaise for up to 1 week) • Prepare Oysters Rockefeller and bake • Fry frites • Shuck fresh oysters and dress with mignonette • Serve frites with mayonnaise

CLASSIC OYSTERS ROCKEFELLER

1 tsp + 1 Tbsp butter (divided)
10 oz bag of spinach, washed
6 slices bacon, diced
1 shallot, finely diced
¼ cup white wine
1 cup heavy cream
pinch of nutmeg
freshly ground black pepper
1 Tbsp Pernod (optional)
1 egg yolk
½ cup freshly grated Parmesan
   (divided)
16 oysters, scrubbed
10 cups kosher salt for baking and
   serving (about 3 lb)
¼ cup breadcrumbs

In a large skillet, heat 1 tsp butter over medium heat. Add spinach and cook for 3 to 4 minutes, or until spinach has wilted. Drain, squeezing out extra liquid, and coarsely chop. Set aside.

In a separate medium skillet, sauté bacon over medium heat, 5 to 6 minutes, or until fat has rendered. Remove all bacon and extra fat, leaving 1 Tbsp bacon fat in the pan. Reserve bacon.

Add 1 Tbsp butter to remaining bacon fat and melt. Add shallot and sweat 3 to 4 minutes, or until translucent. Add white wine to deglaze the pan and stir until pan is almost dry, 2 to 3 minutes. Add cream, nutmeg, and black pepper. Allow liquid to reduce by half, approximately 3 minutes. Add Pernod and remove from heat.

Add chopped, wilted spinach to cream mixture and season with pepper. Stir in egg yolk and combine well. Add ¼ cup Parmesan.

Preheat oven to 400°F.

Shuck oysters. Using a towel, hold oyster flat on work surface, flat shell up. Insert tip of oyster knife into hinge and twist to open shell. Slide knife along inside of upper shell to free oyster from shell; discard upper shell. Slide knife under oyster to free from lower shell; leave in shell. Repeat with remaining oysters.

To assemble oysters, spread about 5 cups kosher salt in a large, shallow, ovenproof baking pan. Nestle oysters in their shell in the salt. Spoon spinach mixture evenly over oysters, and top each oyster with 1 tsp breadcrumbs and 1 tsp Parmesan. Bake oysters in preheated oven for 5 to 6 minutes, or until breadcrumbs are golden.

When oysters come out of the oven, sprinkle each with reserved bacon. Serve warm oysters in shells, nestled in remaining kosher salt (about 5 cups), on a platter.

OYSTERS STRAIGHT-UP WITH MIGNONETTE

½ cup red wine
¼ cup red wine vinegar
2 Tbsp minced shallots
2 tsp freshly ground black pepper
16 oysters, scrubbed
¼ cup chopped fresh chives

To make the mignonette, combine red wine, red wine vinegar, shallots, and pepper in a bowl.

Shuck the oysters.

Place oysters on a large serving tray. Spoon mignonette over oysters. Garnish with chives.

HOMEMADE FRITES

2 pounds Idaho, russet, or Yukon
   Gold potatoes
3–4 cups vegetable oil for frying
salt

Cut potatoes into ⅓-inch matchsticks. Soak in cold water for 10 minutes. Dry all the pieces thoroughly with a clean dish towel (to prevent oil from splattering).

Pour enough oil into a large heavy-bottomed pot to reach at least halfway up the sides of the pot. Heat oil to 360°F. When oil is hot, fry potatoes, in batches, for 3 to 4 minutes, or until golden brown.

Drain on paper towels. Sprinkle with salt.

LEMON ROSEMARY MAYONNAISE

1 cup mayonnaise
1 Tbsp finely chopped rosemary
1 Tbsp lemon juice
1 tsp lemon zest

Combine mayonnaise, rosemary, lemon juice, and zest in a medium bowl and mix well. Keep refrigerated.

133

PASTA

Dried pasta is a staple in my house. There are so many different styles, brands, and varieties out there that it can be hard to navigate through them. One trick is to remember that different pastas are made to complement different styles of sauce. Linguine for example, is the perfect shape for a

rich, creamy alfredo sauce. On the other hand, rigatoni's large tubes are great for picking up a thick, chunky meat sauce. As far as brands go, experiment until you find your favourite.

When you're cooking pasta, it's crucial to salt the water. This allows the seasoning to cook right into

TAGLIATELLE WITH BOLOGNESE SAUCE · BRAISED FENNEL

Tagliatelle Bolognese is a rich, hearty dish and one of my favourite pasta meals. A staple in the cuisine of the Bologna region of Northern Italy, Bolognese is a meat sauce that usually includes a nominal amount of tomato paste.

Even the most traditional recipes for Bolognese vary slightly, although they all share some familiar ingredients: ground beef, pork, veal, pancetta, carrot, onion, wine, and tomato paste. The sauce is usually finished with a small amount of cream or milk, which lightens the sauce and is thought to tenderize the ground meats.

When making Bolognese, it's crucial to brown and break up the ground meats as they cook in order to develop maximum flavour. The meat will go through two obvious stages. First, as the meat begins to cook, the water content steams and reduces away, turning the meat a rather unpleasant opaque grey colour. It's unavoidable. It's imperative to take it past this stage by cooking and breaking up the meat until it caramelizes, turns crispy, and becomes deep brown. That's when the real depth of flavour begins to take shape.

Breaking up the meat as it colours also makes for a smooth uniform sauce that can easily adhere to the tender ribbons of tagliatelle.

Even the most discerning *nonna* will love this Italian dish. *{Serves 4}*

TAGLIATELLE WITH BOLOGNESE SAUCE

Bolognese sauce

4 cups beef stock
3 cups red wine
¼ cup dried porcini mushrooms, finely chopped
2 Tbsp olive oil (divided)
⅓ lb ground veal
⅓ lb ground pork
⅓ lb ground beef
2 Tbsp diced pancetta (about one ½-inch slice)
1 bay leaf
2 cloves garlic
½ onion, diced
½ carrot, diced
2 Tbsp tomato paste
prosciutto ends (optional)
Parmesan rind (optional)
salt and pepper
pinch of nutmeg
½ cup cream (10%)

Pasta

1 lb dry tagliatelle
¼ cup grated Parmesan
olive oil
freshly ground black pepper

Heat beef stock in a pot and leave on stove at a simmer. In a separate, small saucepan, bring red wine to a boil and then down to a simmer. Add chopped porcini mushrooms to rehydrate for approximately 5 minutes.

Heat 1 Tbsp olive oil in a heavy skillet. Add ground meats and gently fry until excess liquid cooks out and meat is well browned, about 6 to 8 minutes, draining excess fat if necessary. Meanwhile, heat remaining 1 Tbsp olive oil in another large heavy-bottomed saucepan over medium heat. Fry pancetta until golden and crispy. Add bay leaf, garlic, onion, and carrot, and sweat until soft. Add tomato paste and stir to *cook out*, about 3 minutes (see page 86).

Add browned meats to saucepan containing pancetta and softened vegetables. Pour in wine and porcini, and bring back up to a low simmer. Add warmed beef stock, prosciutto, and Parmesan rind. Season sauce lightly with salt, pepper, and nutmeg. Simmer on low, stirring occasionally, until sauce is reduced and thick, about

10 to 15 minutes. Just before serving, add cream and stir just to warm through. Adjust seasoning with more salt and pepper, if necessary.

Cook pasta according to package instructions. Toss drained pasta with 1 cup of sauce. Divide dressed pasta evenly among serving plates and spoon remaining sauce overtop. Garnish with grated Parmesan, olive oil, and freshly ground black pepper.

BRAISED FENNEL

2 fennel bulbs
4 Tbsp olive oil (divided)
1 tsp fennel seed
1½ cups chicken stock
½ cup white wine
1 bay leaf
salt and pepper

Preheat oven to 450°F.

Trim any tough or discoloured edges or tips from fennel bulbs. Cut bulbs into six wedges, leaving core intact. Roughly chop and reserve 2 Tbsp fronds.

Heat 2 Tbsp olive oil in a large ovenproof skillet over medium-high heat until hot, but not smoking, then brown fennel slices well, turning over once, about 3 to 4 minutes in total.

Add fennel seed, chicken stock, white wine, and remaining 2 Tbsp olive oil. Braise, partially covered, in preheated oven until fennel is tender, about 15 to 20 minutes. Sprinkle with fennel fronds and season with salt and pepper.

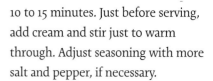

137

PEARS

With its sweet, juicy taste and the soft, buttery texture of its flesh, it's really no wonder the pear was once referred to as a "gift of the gods."

There are over five thousand varieties of pear, which range in colour from green to yellow and red to brown. Cultivated for over three thousand years in Asia, pears were brought to the New World by early French colonists. The fruit has flourished in North American climates, where the most common varieties are Bosc, Bartlett, and Anjou.

Fresh pears should be firm but not overly hard. They should have smooth skin free of bruises, soft spots, and mould. The flesh is usually white to

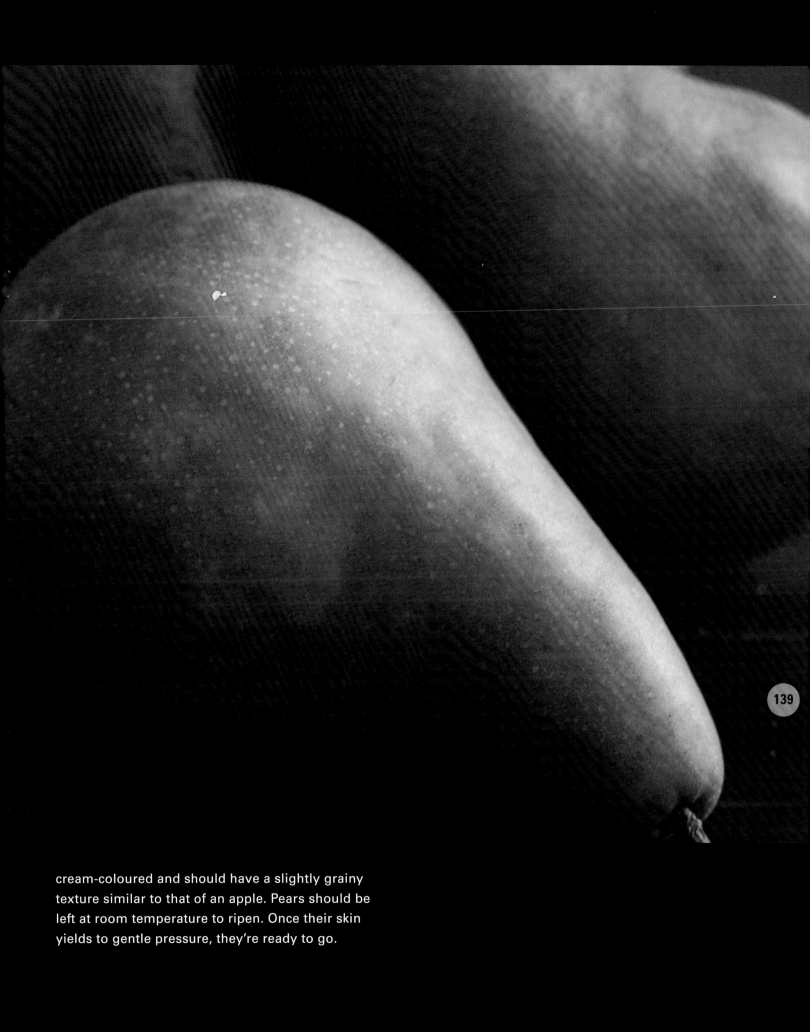

cream-coloured and should have a slightly grainy
texture similar to that of an apple. Pears should be
left at room temperature to ripen. Once their skin
yields to gentle pressure, they're ready to go.

PAN-FRIED CORNISH ROCK HEN WITH MUSTARD AND LEMON · **CELERIAC PURÉE** · PEAR AND RAW MUSHROOM SALAD WITH TOASTED WALNUTS AND THYME · **ROASTED PEARS WITH ROSEMARY** · CARAMELIZED ONIONS · **BLUE CHEESE SAUCE**

PAN-FRIED CORNISH ROCK HEN WITH MUSTARD AND LEMON

2 Cornish hens
2 Tbsp olive oil
1 Tbsp white wine vinegar
4 fresh bay leaves
2 Tbsp Dijon mustard
2 cloves garlic, crushed
1 tsp lemon zest
1 tsp freshly ground black pepper
2 Tbsp grape seed oil (divided)
salt

Cut down backbone of each hen and flip them over. Split each hen in half through breast cavity, creating 4 pieces.

In a large bowl, mix olive oil, white wine vinegar, bay leaves, Dijon mustard, garlic, lemon zest, and black pepper. Add Cornish hens and marinate for at least 20 minutes, and up to 60 minutes, in the refrigerator.

Preheat oven to 425°F.

In 2 large ovenproof skillets, heat grape seed oil over medium-high heat. Season hen pieces generously with salt. Sear hens, skin side down, 2 to 3 minutes, or until lightly browned. Flip and sear another 1 to 2 minutes, basting meat with extra oil in pan. Flip hens back to skin side down and place in preheated oven for 15 to 18 minutes, or until cooked through.

CELERIAC PURÉE

2 Yukon Gold potatoes, peeled and chopped
1 celeriac bulb, peeled and chopped
1 bay leaf
½ cup whipping cream (35%)
¼ cup butter
salt and pepper

Place potatoes and celeriac in a large pot of cold water and bring to a boil. Reduce heat and simmer 35 to 45 minutes, or until vegetables are tender.

Drain vegetables and transfer to a bowl of a stand mixer. Add whipping cream and butter and whisk until smooth. Season with salt and pepper.

PEAR AND RAW MUSHROOM SALAD WITH TOASTED WALNUTS AND THYME

½ lb king oyster mushrooms, thinly sliced (or cremini mushrooms)
juice of 1 lemon
2 Forelle pears, cut into ¼-inch pieces
4 radishes, julienned
⅓ cup chopped walnuts, toasted
2 Tbsp chopped thyme
olive oil, for drizzling
salt and pepper

Divide sliced mushrooms among 4 plates. Drizzle with half of lemon juice. Top with pears, radishes, walnuts, and thyme. Drizzle with remaining lemon juice and olive oil, and season with salt and pepper.

ROASTED PEARS WITH ROSEMARY

2 Bosc pears, cut into 6 wedges
2 Tbsp olive oil
2 Tbsp sugar
1 Tbsp butter
½ tsp freshly ground black pepper
2 sprigs rosemary
pinch of salt

Preheat oven to 425°F.

In a small cast iron skillet, toss all ingredients together. Transfer to preheated oven and roast 20 minutes, or until pears are soft and golden brown.

CARAMELIZED ONIONS

2 Tbsp butter
2 Tbsp olive oil
2 Vidalia onions, thinly sliced
salt and pepper

In a large skillet, melt butter and olive oil over medium heat. Add onions and cook, stirring occasionally, until golden brown, about 20 to 25 minutes.

Remove from heat and season with salt and pepper.

BLUE CHEESE SAUCE

1 cup chicken stock
¼ cup white wine
½ cup whipping cream (35%)
½ cup crumbled blue cheese
1 Tbsp butter

In a small saucepan, bring chicken stock and white wine to a boil. Reduce heat and simmer until liquid has reduced by half, about 8 to 10 minutes.

Stir in whipping cream and simmer 2 to 3 minutes. Add blue cheese and stir to combine.

Remove from heat and stir in butter to finish sauce.

141

POMEGRANATES

The pomegranate is one of the most visually
stunning fruits. The outside appears relatively
simple, but the inside is packed with clusters of
ruby-red, glistening arils, each one plump with
sweet, tangy juice. In the centre of each aril is a
small, relatively tender seed. These seeds are

edible and provide a good source of fibre.
However, the white membrane of the pomegranate, which surrounds the arils, is very bitter
and inedible.

Pomegranates are delicious fresh, but there are
processed forms of pomegranates that offer an

amazing spectrum of flavour—syrup, molasses, and vinegar, for example.

The commercial season for pomegranates is October through January, making them an exotic and colourful way to spruce up a winter meal. Unlike many other fruits, pomegranates are only picked once they're fully ripe, so pomegranates in the grocery store and market are ready to be enjoyed. When choosing a fresh pomegranate, look for fruit that is unblemished by cuts or soft spots and surprisingly heavy for its size.

GRILLED LAMB LOIN WITH SPICED POMEGRANATE GLAZE · QUINOA PILAF WITH LEMON AND ZUCCHINI · POMEGRANATE SALAD WITH FETA AND FRESH MINT

GRILLED LAMB LOIN WITH SPICED POMEGRANATE GLAZE

1 Tbsp whole black peppercorns
1 Tbsp whole allspice
¼ tsp ground cinnamon
½ cup pomegranate molasses
2 lamb loins, trimmed and cleaned
salt

In a mortar and pestle or spice grinder, grind black peppercorns, allspice, and cinnamon. In a small bowl, combine pomegranate molasses with spice mixture. Spread glaze over lamb, cover with plastic wrap, and marinate in the refrigerator for 30 minutes.

Preheat barbecue grill to medium-high. Season lamb with salt and grill on barbecue for 3–4 minutes. Flip meat and grill an additional 3–4 minutes, basting with additional leftover glaze. Remove meat from heat and let rest 3–5 minutes. Slice lamb against the grain.

QUINOA PILAF WITH LEMON AND ZUCCHINI

1 cup quinoa
2 Tbsp olive oil
5 green onions, chopped, white and green parts separate
1 clove garlic, finely chopped
1 medium zucchini, diced
2 tsp lemon juice
zest of 1 lemon
salt and pepper

In a medium pot, bring 8 cups of salted water to a boil. Add quinoa and cook for 12 minutes, or until tender. Drain in colander and rinse with cold water.

In a large skillet, heat olive oil over medium heat. Add the whites of the green onion and garlic. Sauté 1 minute, or until soft and translucent.

Add zucchini and cook 3–4 minutes, or until tender. Add cooked quinoa, the greens of the green onion, lemon juice, and zest. Season with salt and pepper. This dish can be served warm or at room temperature.

POMEGRANATE SALAD WITH FETA AND FRESH MINT

2 large pomegranates, seeds only
½ cup crumbled feta
½ cup hulled green pumpkin seeds (pepitas), toasted
2 Tbsp coarsely chopped fresh mint

In a small bowl, combine pomegranate seeds, crumbled feta, and pumpkin seeds. Toss to combine. Before serving, sprinkle with fresh mint.

145

PRIME RIB

Prime rib is one of the most flavourful cuts of meat available. It has a naturally high amount of marbled fat, which gives the meat its flavour and keeps it moist and juicy while cooking. Prime rib can either be cut into steaks (rib eyes) or roasted whole and then carved. There are benefits to cooking prime rib as a roast instead of as individual steaks. It requires slow cooking, which results in super-tender, evenly cooked, juicy meat.

A whole prime rib is a very large roast. As a result, it is a staple at banquets and in large hotel buffets, but not a common choice for the home cook. It is simply too large for the average household oven. Prime rib can, however, be cut

SLOW-ROASTED PRIME RIB WITH BUTTON MUSHROOMS AND GLAZED BABY ONIONS · **HORSERADISH BUTTERMILK MASHED POTATOES** · YORKSHIRE PUDDING

This main is close to my heart. During my time cooking in London, brasserie-style foods like this were regularly on the menu. Food is about comfort and enjoyment, and this dish is my kind of comfort food. I absolutely love how the onions and mushrooms complement the beef and soak up all its juices.

Beef and horseradish are a classic flavour pairing. My father always had his own private reserve of horseradish in the fridge just for roast night. And what's a great roast without a great Yorkshire pudding? The English classic is the perfect vehicle to soak up every last bit of sauce on any plate. This dish is simplicity at its finest; a perfect example of how humble ingredients can combine to make a satisfying meal. I've always said that my time cooking in London was more valuable than any other, and it's because of dishes like this. *(Serves 4)*

[TIMING IS EVERYTHING]

Boil potatoes • Sear and roast meat • Prepare Yorkshire Pudding batter and cream mixture for mash • When potatoes are tender, complete mash and keep warm • Remove prime rib from oven and set aside to rest • Bake Yorkshire Puddings • Finish sauce for roast • Slice roast against the grain and serve with vegetables and pan sauce • Remove puddings from oven just before serving

SLOW-ROASTED PRIME RIB WITH BUTTON MUSHROOMS AND GLAZED BABY ONIONS

one 3 lb prime rib roast
1 Tbsp kosher salt
1 Tbsp coarsely ground pepper
1 Tbsp vegetable oil
4 whole garlic cloves, peeled
12 cipollini or pearl onions, peeled
1 lb button mushrooms
5 sprigs thyme
½ cup white wine
½ cup beef stock
1 Tbsp butter

Preheat oven to 350°F.

Sprinkle meat with salt and pepper. In a large ovenproof sauté pan, heat vegetable oil over medium-high heat. Sear meat for 3 to 5 minutes per side, or until golden brown on all sides. Add garlic, onions, mushrooms, and thyme. Cook 1 to 2 minutes more.

Transfer pan to preheated oven and roast until meat is cooked to medium, 45 to 60 minutes. Remove from oven and transfer meat to another dish. Let meat rest 5 to 10 minutes.

Add white wine to sauté pan and simmer over medium heat to reduce volume by half. Add beef stock and reduce by half. Add butter and stir gently.

HORSERADISH BUTTERMILK MASHED POTATOES

5 medium Yukon Gold potatoes, peeled and cut into large chunks
½ cup butter
½ cup whipping cream (35%)
½ cup buttermilk
2½ Tbsp prepared horseradish
salt and pepper

Place potatoes in a large pot and cover by 1 inch with cold salted water. Bring to a simmer and cook, uncovered, about 20 minutes, or until tender.

Shortly before potatoes have finished cooking, combine butter, whipping cream, buttermilk, and horseradish in a small saucepan. Simmer mixture over medium heat.

Drain potatoes well in a colander and return to pot along with hot cream mixture; season with salt and pepper. Mash with a potato masher until well combined.

Season with more salt and pepper if necessary. Serve immediately or keep hot, uncovered, in a double boiler.

YORKSHIRE PUDDING

3 large eggs
1 cup whole milk
1 cup all-purpose flour
pinch of salt
⅓ cup clarified butter (or pan drippings from the prime rib roast)

In a medium bowl, whisk eggs. Gradually whisk in milk. Sift flour and salt into egg mixture and whisk until well blended and smooth. Let batter stand at room temperature at least 30 minutes. Transfer to large measuring cup or pitcher with a spout for easy pouring.

Preheat oven to 450°F.

Heat a 12-cup muffin tin in oven for 10 minutes. Pour about 1 tsp melted clarified butter (or pan drippings) into each muffin cup. Return pan to oven until fat is hot, about 6 to 8 minutes. Re-whisk batter and pour it evenly into the muffin cups onto the hot fat. (The key to getting these puddings to puff up is to make sure that the fat is very hot when you add the batter.) Bake until puddings are golden and puffy, about 12 to 15 minutes. Puddings will sink slightly in centre. Serve immediately out of oven.

149

PROSCIUTTO

Prosciutto is the Italian word for "ham." In English, however, it refers to a specific variety of ham made from salt-cured pork leg. This means that prosciutto has a higher salt content than traditional cooked ham, which is important to take into account when pairing it with other foods.

Good-quality prosciutto has good colour and should be streaked with soft, white, buttery fat. The really good stuff almost melts in your mouth. For the best flavour it's important to slice prosciutto thinly, which keeps it tender and delicate. It's best done on a meat slicer, and any

PROSCIUTTO-WRAPPED HALIBUT
WITH PUTTANESCA SAUCE · LEMON ORZO WITH
PARSLEY AND OLIVE OIL · GRILLED FENNEL

Besides being delicious on its own, prosciutto's salty flavour and buttery fat make it perfect for wrapping around mild white fish like halibut. Lean, light, and flaky, halibut benefits from both the flavour of the prosciutto and its soft, white fat, which melts into the fish as it cooks and keeps it moist.

How puttanesca sauce came to be named is a bit of a funny story. *Pasta alla Puttanesca* roughly translates to "pasta the way a prostitute would make it." Yes, the name of this sauce originates from the ladies of the night in old-world Naples.

Since the prosciutto, capers, and olives in the sauce are all quite salty, be mindful of how much additional salt you season it with.

The sauce and the fish in this main are very flavourful, so I've kept the sides nice and simple. A form of pasta, orzo is nice simply dressed with olive oil, lemon, and fresh herbs and chilled as a salad. Grilled fennel is an interesting way to shake up a standard-issue side of vegetables. *{Serves 4}*

PROSCIUTTO-WRAPPED HALIBUT WITH PUTTANESCA SAUCE

Halibut

four 6 oz halibut fillets
freshly ground black pepper
4 sprigs thyme
4 pieces thinly sliced prosciutto
2 Tbsp olive oil

Sauce

1 Tbsp olive oil
¼ cup diced red onion
1 clove garlic, chopped
1 Tbsp capers, rinsed and drained
1 bay leaf
2 Tbsp sliced green olives
2 Tbsp white wine
1 pint cherry or grape tomatoes
2 Tbsp chopped parsley

Preheat oven to 400°F.

Season fillets with pepper; place 1 thyme sprig on top of each and wrap each fillet with prosciutto. Heat olive oil in a large cast iron or heavy-bottomed pan over medium-high heat. When oil starts to smoke, add fish, placing prosciutto seam side down. Sear on all sides until prosciutto is coloured and crispy. Transfer to a plate and keep warm.

To prepare sauce, heat 1 Tbsp olive oil in same pan over medium-high heat. Add red onion, garlic, capers, and bay leaf, and sauté until onion is lightly coloured. Add olives and white wine. Bring to a simmer, add tomatoes, and return fish to pan. Place pan in oven and cook until fish is tender and cooked through, about 5 minutes. Top with parsley.

LEMON ORZO WITH PARSLEY AND OLIVE OIL

2 cups orzo
juice and zest of 1 lemon
1 green onion, chopped
3 Tbsp roughly chopped parsley
2 Tbsp olive oil
salt and pepper

Cook orzo al dente according to package instructions. Drain but do not rinse. In a large bowl, combine warm orzo with lemon juice, zest, green onion, parsley, and olive oil. Season with salt and pepper.

GRILLED FENNEL

1 fennel bulb
juice of 1 orange
2 Tbsp olive oil
freshly ground pepper
salt

Slice fennel lengthwise into four ½-inch-thick slices. Combine orange juice, olive oil, and pepper in a shallow dish and marinate fennel for 5 to 10 minutes. Turn grill to medium-high. Remove fennel from marinade; salt lightly and grill until marked on both sides, about 3 minutes each side. Return fennel to marinade to keep moist until serving.

153

RAISINS

The practice of drying grapes to preserve them dates back to ancient times. Today, making raisins entails either sun-drying or oven-drying fresh grapes. The result is tangy, chewy, all-natural nuggets of sweetness! Dried fruit is commonly used in North African cuisine because it provides a burst of sweetness and a chewy texture that perfectly complements the fragrant, warm spices used in the region's signature dishes.

Raisins come in an array of colours, including white, green, golden, purple, and black. Popular grape varieties for making raisins include sultana, Malaga, Monukka, Zante currant, Muscat, and Thompson seedless. All varieties should be stored

MOROCCAN SPICED TURKEY TAGINE WITH RAISINS, GINGER, AND ALMONDS · FRUIT AND NUT COUSCOUS WITH MINT · YOGURT DIP

Morocco's exciting, exotic cuisine clearly reflects its position as the gateway between Europe and Africa. A classic Moroccan dish, tagine is named after the earthenware pot it's cooked in. Traditionally, tagines are slow-cooked stews with beef or lamb, aromatic spices, vegetables, olives, dried fruits, nuts, and a sauce or braising liquid. Inspired by the exotic flavours of North Africa, my version is very traditional except that it features turkey instead of beef or lamb. I find that turkey's nice, simple taste easily absorbs the tagine's aromatic spices (coriander, cumin, freshly ground black pepper, garlic, and ginger). I also love to add pine nuts and almonds for their crunchy textures and raisins for a burst of sweetness. The light Fruit and Nut Couscous with Mint is an easy, authentic, and delicious accompaniment to this Moroccan main. *{Serves 4}*

MOROCCAN SPICED TURKEY TAGINE WITH RAISINS, GINGER, AND ALMONDS

Turkey

1 clove garlic, minced
1 Tbsp ground coriander
½ tsp ground cumin
½ tsp freshly ground black pepper
½ tsp ground ginger
1½ lb boneless, skinless dark turkey or chicken meat (from leg or thigh), cut into large bite-sized pieces
1 Tbsp olive oil
½ cup white wine
1¼ cups chicken stock

Tagine

1 Tbsp olive oil
12 red pearl onions or shallots, peeled and cut in half
2 cloves garlic, crushed
4 cloves
½ tsp fennel seeds
1-inch piece ginger, peeled
1 bay leaf
1 cinnamon stick
⅓ cup capers
½ cup golden raisins, plus extra for garnish
¼ cup ground almonds
¼ cup sliced almonds
2 Tbsp chopped cilantro stems
zest of 1 lemon
chopped cilantro, for garnish

Preheat oven to 350°F.

To prepare the turkey, combine garlic, coriander, cumin, black pepper, and ginger in a medium bowl. Add turkey pieces and toss to coat. Use immediately or marinate for 15 to 20 minutes in the refrigerator.

In a large skillet, heat olive oil over medium-high heat. Add spiced turkey and sear until golden on all sides (you may need to do this in batches). Add white wine and allow liquid to reduce by half, about 2 to 3 minutes. Add chicken stock and simmer 5 minutes, or until slightly thickened.

In a tagine pot, heat 1 Tbsp olive oil over medium heat. Add pearl onions and garlic and sauté 3 to 5 minutes, or until golden. Add cloves, fennel seeds, ginger, bay leaf, and cinnamon stick. Allow spices to toast slightly. Add capers and raisins. Add ground and sliced almonds and stir to combine.

Add seared turkey and its liquid to tagine and bring to a simmer. Add cilantro stems and lemon zest. Transfer to preheated oven and cook for 30 to 40 minutes, or until turkey is cooked through and mixture has thickened. Garnish with fresh cilantro and raisins.

FRUIT AND NUT COUSCOUS WITH MINT

1 cup couscous
1½ cups water
1 cup raisins
½ cups sliced almonds, toasted
⅓ cup pine nuts, toasted
3 green onions, sliced
¼ cup chopped cilantro
¼ cup chopped mint
¼ cup olive oil
2 Tbsp white wine vinegar
1 clove garlic, minced
1½ tsp cinnamon
juice of 1 lemon
salt and pepper

Place couscous in a medium bowl. In a medium saucepan, bring water to a boil. Add raisins and return to boil. Remove from heat and pour liquid over couscous. Cover and let stand for 5 to 10 minutes. Fluff couscous with a fork and transfer to a shallow baking pan to cool as quickly as possible. Cool couscous completely and break up any large lumps. Stir in almonds, pine nuts, green onions, cilantro, and mint.

In a medium bowl, whisk together olive oil, white wine vinegar, garlic, cinnamon, and lemon juice. Pour over couscous, stir, and season with salt and pepper.

YOGURT DIP

1 cup plain yogurt
2 Tbsp chopped cilantro
1 Tbsp honey

In a small bowl, combine all ingredients. Refrigerate.

157

RICOTTA

Ricotta is not technically a cheese; it is actually made from the whey that gets drained off in the process of making cheese like provolone and mozzarella. The name *ricotta* literally translates to "re-cooked," which refers to the fact that the curd is actually cooked twice in the manufacturing process.

You can find ricotta at most markets and grocers, and delicatessens usually have the best stuff.

Good-quality, fresh ricotta should be brilliant white without any yellowish tinges. It should smell mildly sweet. If it doesn't, it's probably seen better days and it's time to say goodbye. On average,

RICOTTA AND SPINACH
STUFFED CANNELLONI · INSALATA VERDE

Baked pastas have always been popular in Italy and make delectable, casual family food that can be easily shared. While the best-known baked pasta dish is probably lasagna, this is right behind in terms of popularity.

Making your own pasta is rewarding and moderately easy. It's the kind of thing you can only get better at with practice.

Taking that into account, if you aren't inspired to make your own pasta from scratch, this recipe can be made with fresh pasta sheets (which you can find

in Italian delicatessens) or dried cannelloni tubes. If you do use dried tubes, make sure they have enough tomato sauce and time to fully cook. It will take longer than fresh pasta.

I love the cannelloni filling in this recipe. The classic combination of sweet, creamy ricotta and tender spinach is timeless. The two contrasting sauces are equally nice; one is rich, thick, and velvety, while the other is tangy and acidic. The colours in the finished dish are those of the Italian flag. {Serves 4}

RICOTTA AND SPINACH STUFFED CANNELLONI

Pasta dough

2 cups semolina flour (finely ground)
pinch of salt
1 Tbsp + 1 tsp olive oil
3 whole eggs
3 egg yolks (reserve whites)

For the pasta, place semolina, salt, and olive oil in a food processor and pulse. Add eggs and yolks, one at a time, pulsing in between each addition. Continue to process until ingredients are well combined and dough comes away from the sides of the container. Pulse 1 to 2 minutes to knead dough. Remove dough from processor, roll into a ball, cover, and refrigerate for at least 30 minutes.

When dough is rested, cut into 8 equal pieces. Roll out 4 pieces on a pasta machine, according to machine instructions, on thinnest setting. (Remaining dough can be well wrapped and frozen for later use. To use, defrost in fridge overnight and roll out as above.) Cut each rolled-out piece of dough into three 4-inch squares for a total of 12 squares. Cover with cloth to prevent drying out.

Spinach-ricotta filling

8 oz spinach
1 Tbsp butter
pinch of nutmeg
1 egg
2 cups fresh ricotta
salt and pepper

For the filling, wash and drain spinach, letting some water cling to spinach leaves. In a medium skillet, melt butter over medium-high heat. Add spinach and cook until leaves are wilted and soft. Season with nutmeg. Drain cooked spinach in a colander, pressing down firmly to remove excess liquid. Finely chop drained spinach and gently combine with egg and ricotta in a large bowl. Season mixture with salt and pepper.

Béchamel sauce

2 Tbsp butter
2 Tbsp flour
1¼ cups milk
1 bay leaf
salt and pepper

Melt butter in a heavy-bottomed saucepan. Stir in flour and cook, stirring constantly, until the paste cooks and bubbles a bit but does not colour, about 2 minutes. Stream milk in, whisking as sauce thickens. Bring to a low simmer. Add bay leaf and salt and pepper. Lower heat and cook, stirring, for 2 to 3 minutes more. Remove from heat and cover with plastic wrap.

Tomato sauce

3 Tbsp olive oil
2 cloves garlic, minced
one 710 mL jar good-quality, Italian-brand strained tomatoes
salt and pepper
3 Tbsp torn basil leaves

Heat olive oil and garlic in a pot over medium heat. Gently fry garlic for 1 minute; add strained tomatoes. Simmer gently about 10 minutes. Season sauce with salt and pepper. Remove from heat and stir in torn basil leaves.

Assembly

1 cup grated Parmesan
1 cup shredded mozzarella
extra ricotta (reserved from tub)
3 egg whites (reserved from pasta dough recipe)

Preheat oven to 375°F.

To assemble, lay pasta squares on a lightly floured surface. Pipe or spoon about 2 Tbsp of spinach-ricotta filling evenly along bottom edge of each square. Brush egg white along top edge of square. Gently roll bottom edge up and around to form a tube shape. Repeat with all pasta squares.

Spread ¼ cup tomato sauce on bottom of a 9- × 13-inch ovenproof dish. Arrange filled cannelloni on top and pour béchamel sauce over. Spoon over remaining tomato sauce just to cover. Sprinkle Parmesan, mozzarella, and ricotta on top and bake until tomato sauce is bubbling around edges, about 15 to 20 minutes.

INSALATA VERDE

6 cups mixed greens, washed and dried
1 Tbsp extra virgin olive oil
2 tsp good-quality white wine vinegar
salt and pepper
3 Tbsp shaved Parmesan to garnish, if desired

Toss greens well with oil, vinegar, and salt and pepper. Garnish with Parmesan shavings.

RUSSET POTATOES

The potato is the world's most popular and widely consumed vegetable. Of the potato's many varieties, the russet is one of the most common in North American cuisine. Russet potatoes can be mashed, smashed, baked, boiled, roasted, or fried. On their own, they are low in calories and

loaded with nutrients. They're available absolutely everywhere. When you're purchasing russets, look for hard, unblemished potatoes with a reddish brown skin or "jacket."

Russet potatoes are incredibly versatile. They are high in starch, which makes them great for baking

PAN-FRIED TRI-TIP STEAK · HERBED
BUTTER · THE WORLD'S FINEST SCALLOPED POTATOES · BAKED
ASPARAGUS WITH MARINATED TOMATOES

This main is really a collection of my favourite recipes to cook at home. All the dishes offer simple flavour combinations and are tasty and easy to prepare.

These scalloped potatoes really are the best in the world. I learned how to make them at a classic French restaurant in England. The French call them *gratin dauphinoise*. They're amazing because of the russet potato's high starch content and a great little technique of cooking the potatoes in cream. The starch thickens the cream mixture and gives it a velvety texture. These potatoes represent true comfort food to me. I recommend ketchup.

For years, the beef tri-tip or triangle roast, which sits at the bottom of the sirloin, was ground into hamburger. There is only one tri-tip per side of beef, and back when butchers carved their own meat it was considered a waste of display space to sell the tri-tip by itself. Now that the carving is done by packers, you are much more likely to find the tri-tip at your local butcher. If you don't, ask for it. This often-overlooked piece of meat is not only relatively inexpensive, but also very flavourful and quite lean, making it a favourite of those in the know. *{Serves 4}*

[TIMING IS EVERYTHING]

Prepare flavoured butter and place in fridge or freezer to set (can also be made up to 1 month ahead and frozen) • Prepare and bake scalloped potatoes • Prepare asparagus and bake • Sear steaks • Cool potatoes • Allow steak to rest • Prepare tomato topping for asparagus

PAN-FRIED TRI-TIP STEAK

four 5–6 oz tri-tip steaks
salt and pepper
2 Tbsp olive oil

Preheat oven to 350°F.

Pat meat dry and season with salt and pepper. Heat oil in a cast iron skillet over medium-high heat. When pan is hot, add meat and sear 2 minutes per side, or until golden brown.

Transfer pan to preheated oven and cook 3 to 4 minutes more, or until medium-rare.

Let meat rest 2 to 3 minutes and serve with Herbed Butter.

HERBED BUTTER

1 lb salted butter
1 bunch flat leaf parsley, washed and dried
1 bunch chives, washed and dried
1 Tbsp Worcestershire sauce
1 tsp hot sauce
juice of ½ lemon

In a medium saucepan, melt butter over medium heat. Let cool slightly.

In a blender, combine herbs, Worcestershire sauce, hot sauce, and lemon juice. Slowly add melted butter and blend until incorporated. Do not overmix or herbs will bruise. Transfer mixture to a metal bowl, and place bowl in an ice bath. Whisk until mixture has cooled and emulsified. Place mixture in freezer for 5 minutes.

Remove from freezer and continue mixing until butter is thick and reconstituted.

Divide mixture in half. Place half of butter on a large piece of plastic wrap. Roll tightly into a log. Repeat with other half. Store in refrigerator until use.

THE WORLD'S FINEST SCALLOPED POTATOES

5 Tbsp butter (divided)
2 cups half and half cream
2 cloves garlic, finely chopped
pinch of nutmeg
2 sprigs rosemary, chopped
salt and pepper
5 large russet potatoes, peeled and sliced into ⅛-inch-thick rounds
1 cup shredded cheddar cheese

Preheat oven to 400°F. Grease the inside of an 8- x 8-inch baking dish with 1 Tbsp butter.

In a large pot set over medium heat, melt remaining butter with cream, garlic, nutmeg, and rosemary. Season with salt and pepper. Add potatoes and bring to a boil. Cook for 8 to 10 minutes, or until potatoes are slightly tender.

Transfer mixture to prepared baking dish, smoothing as much as possible. Cover potatoes with grated cheese and bake for 20 to 30 minutes, or until golden brown. Let potatoes cool slightly before serving.

BAKED ASPARAGUS WITH MARINATED TOMATOES

1 lb asparagus, trimmed
2 slices Herbed Butter, approximately ⅛ inch thick
¼ cup breadcrumbs
¼ cup grated Parmesan
1 Tbsp plus 1 tsp olive oil (divided)
3–4 plum tomatoes, coarsely chopped
1 shallot, finely chopped
½ tsp red wine vinegar
salt and pepper

Preheat oven to 400°F.

Place asparagus in an ovenproof ceramic dish. Top with Herbed Butter. Sprinkle with breadcrumbs and Parmesan. Drizzle with 1 Tbsp olive oil and salt and pepper.

Bake in preheated oven for 10 to 12 minutes, or until crust is golden brown and crispy.

Meanwhile, in a medium bowl, combine tomatoes, shallot, remaining 1 tsp olive oil, red wine vinegar, and salt and pepper. Remove asparagus from oven and serve with marinated tomatoes.

165

SAFFRON

Saffron is harvested from the stigma of the purple crocus flower. One crocus produces about three or four stigmas, each of which has to be hand-picked. It takes around fifteen thousand saffron stigmas to make up a single ounce of spice—that's almost a quarter million to make up a pound. This painstaking process, coupled with saffron's unique flavour and vibrant colour, make it the world's most expensive spice.

Although it is expensive, saffron has such an intense taste that it only takes a few threads to flavour an entire meal. Saffron is great in many recipes, from a classic Spanish paella to a great risotto Milanese. It doesn't stop with savoury

foods—saffron is also great in pastries. Many Middle Eastern sweets feature its unmistakable taste and incredible colour.

Saffron should be kept in an airtight container in the pantry and will be good for up to for six months. When it comes time to cook with saffron, try steeping the threads in a small amount of warm white wine, broth, stock, lemon juice, or water, which will release its flavour and colour.

PAELLA LIKE THEY MAKE IT IN
SPAIN · SANGRIA CAVA

Named after the wide shallow pan in which it's traditionally cooked, paella is a well-known Spanish rice dish originating from Valencia. The key players are paella rice (a short-grain variety) saffron, chorizo, and a varying assortment of meats and fish. I love this one-pot wonder because it's easy to make and has a killer flavour—it's an ideal dish to share among friends. I like to make this up at the cabin or on camping trips. Once you have it down, you can even make it over an open fire to bring its authentic spirit home.

The technique with this dish is simple. The goal is to stagger the addition of each ingredient so that by the time the rice is tender all of the other ingredients are perfectly cooked. The bonus is that by cooking everything in one pan, the flavours of the different components blend together wonderfully.

Sangria Cava is the perfect drink to sip while enjoying this main. Sangria is generally made with red wine, brandy, soda water, sugar or honey, and loads of fresh fruit. Sangria Cava uses a traditional sparkling white wine in place of the red wine, and makes a unique, crisp drink that pairs perfectly with paella. *{Serves 4}*

PAELLA LIKE THEY MAKE IT IN SPAIN

2 Tbsp olive oil

4 chicken thighs, skin on, excess fat trimmed

½ cup diced chorizo (about one sausage)

½ red onion, diced

3 cloves garlic, chopped

2 cups arborio or Valencia (short-grain) rice

1 tsp sweet smoked paprika

2 tsp saffron

1 bay leaf

1 cup white wine

3 cups chicken stock

salt and pepper

2 small tomatoes, diced

1 lb clams, scrubbed and debearded

1 lb mussels, scrubbed and debearded

12 large shrimp, peeled and deveined

Preheat oven to 450°F.

Heat olive oil in a large, wide oven-proof skillet on medium heat. Sear chicken, skin side down first, until deep golden brown. Set chicken aside. Gently fry chorizo for 1 to 2 minutes, then add onion and garlic and sweat until onion is soft. Add rice and paprika and stir, toasting rice for 3 to 4 minutes.

Add saffron, bay leaf, white wine, and chicken stock; bring to a simmer and season lightly with salt and pepper. Return seared chicken to pan. Add tomatoes and clams. Place in hot oven on middle rack and roast, stirring occasionally, until rice is three-quarters done, about 15 minutes. Add mussels and shrimp to pan and continue to roast until mussels open and cook through, about 6 to 8 minutes. Remove from heat and season with additional salt and pepper.

SANGRIA CAVA

1 orange, sliced

1 lemon, sliced

1 lime, sliced

1 cup halved strawberries (or diced peaches or nectarines)

3 Tbsp brandy

3 Tbsp sugar

one 750 mL bottle cava (Spanish sparkling wine)

Combine orange, lemon, and lime slices with strawberries and brandy in a pitcher. Add sugar and toss to coat; let stand at least five minutes. Pour cold sparkling wine over, stir to combine flavours, and serve immediately.

SESAME SEEDS

Sesame seeds may seem like a humble little ingredient, but they're actually loaded with rich, nutty flavour and extremely high in protein. The seeds' slightly sweet, fragrant, and extremely nutty oil gives them their unique flavour. These seeds can be pressed into oil or ground into a purée known as tahini, which has a similar texture to peanut butter and is a common ingredient in hummus.

There are many different varieties of sesame seeds. The most common are white and charcoal black, which are popular in the Far East. Beside the obvious aesthetic differences, the two varieties are very similar. Sesame seeds of all varieties

are truly amazing and it's their versatility that
really sets them apart. They're a staple in both
sweet and savoury dishes, widely used in breads
(bagels, buns, crackers, and loaves) and a variety
of pastries.

SESAME-CRUSTED AHI TUNA · SEARED TOFU IN SOY-MIRIN SAUCE · GOMAE SALAD · MARINATED RADISHES

I absolutely love Japanese food. The knife techniques in Japanese cuisine are surpassed by none and give finished dishes a clean, artistic look. But presentation isn't everything, and the Japanese certainly don't disappoint on taste. The cuisine uses a unique blend of sweet and savoury ingredients that offer bright, bold, and clean flavours. Japanese food never feels too heavy either, because it's all about intense, big-tasting ingredients that are light in texture and consistency—like sesame seeds.

This main combines sesame seeds with the buttery texture of tuna and tofu, spinach, and some

spectacular sauces. A great example of Japanese cuisine, bonito soy sauce is a simple combination of dried tuna flakes, soy sauce, mirin (sweet rice wine), and sesame oil. This dressing works wonders in flavouring tofu.

Tuna is considered a prize fish in Japan. There are many different varieties, but sushi-grade ahi tuna is considered the best. It has an amazingly rich red colour, soft texture, and mild taste. When you're buying ahi tuna, look for a plump, fresh-looking fish with vibrant colours, a clean smell, and closely spaced, undamaged layers of flesh. {Serves 4}

SESAME-CRUSTED AHI TUNA

½ lb sushi-grade tuna, cut into
  1-inch cubes
1 egg white, beaten until frothy
½ cup sesame seeds
1 tsp grape seed oil

Dip one side of tuna into beaten egg white, then into sesame seeds. Repeat with remaining tuna. Leave at room temperature for 15 minutes.

Heat oil in a large non-stick skillet over medium-high heat. Add tuna, seed side down, and sear until lightly coloured, about 1 to 2 minutes. Remove from heat and let sit 1 to 2 minutes. This will allow the temperature of the fish to rise slightly.

SEARED TOFU IN SOY-MIRIN SAUCE

Bonito soy sauce

1 cup loosely packed bonito flakes
½ cup soy sauce
¾ cup mirin
6 Tbsp sake or cooking sake
1 tsp sesame oil

Heat a non-stick pan over medium-high heat. Add bonito flakes and toast 2 to 3 minutes. Remove from heat and crush bonito flakes with fingers.

In a medium bowl, mix soy sauce, mirin, sake, and sesame oil, and stir to combine.

Add bonito flakes to soy mixture and stir to combine.

Chili spice blend

½ nori sheet
1 tsp black sesame seeds
1 tsp white sesame seeds
1 tsp poppy seeds
3 tsp orange or tangerine zest
2 tsp freshly ground black pepper
1 tsp chili powder or red chili flakes

Toast nori sheet over medium-low heat of burner, or in a small skillet. In a mortar and pestle or spice grinder, grind black sesame seeds, white sesame seeds, and poppy seeds together. Crumble nori sheet and add to seed mixture. Add orange zest, pepper, and chili powder, and stir to combine.

Seared tofu

1 block medium tofu, sliced
  horizontally in half and cut into
  quarters
2 egg whites, beaten until frothy
1 Tbsp grape seed oil
2 green onions, sliced
bonito soy sauce
chili spice blend, for garnish

In a shallow bowl, toss tofu in egg whites. Let sit 10 minutes.

In a large non-stick skillet, heat oil over medium-high heat. Add tofu and sear until golden brown, 2 to 3 minutes per side. Remove from pan. Add green onions to skillet and lightly sauté for 1 minute.

Spoon 1 tsp of bonito soy sauce and sautéed green onions over each piece of tofu. Garnish with chili spice blend.

GOMAE SALAD

½ cup sesame seeds, toasted
¼ cup brown sugar
¼ cup tahini
¼ cup sake
3 Tbsp rice wine vinegar
3 Tbsp soy sauce
2 Tbsp mirin
1 tsp sesame oil
½ cup + 2 Tbsp grape seed oil
¼ cup sliced green onions
1 bag spinach, stems removed,
  chopped
pinch of salt

In a spice grinder, or using a mortar and pestle, grind sesame seeds. Transfer to a blender and add brown sugar, tahini, sake, rice wine vinegar, soy sauce, mirin, and sesame oil. Blend at a low speed to combine. Slowly add ½ cup grape seed oil to emulsify dressing.

In a large skillet, heat remaining 2 Tbsp grape seed oil over medium heat. Add green onions and sauté until soft, 2 to 3 minutes. Add spinach and salt and let spinach wilt slightly, 3 to 4 minutes. Remove from heat and toss spinach with dressing.

MARINATED RADISHES

4 radishes, sliced
reserved bonito soy sauce (see left)

Place radish slices in a bowl of ice water to crisp, 5 to 10 minutes. Remove and drain well.

Just before serving, toss radishes with bonito soy sauce.

173

SUN-DRIED TOMATOES

When you're cooking with sun-dried tomatoes, it's important to remember that they have an intense, concentrated flavour. They can't be paired with everything, but when they're matched with complementary flavours the results can be incredible. Try combining sun-dried tomatoes in a food processor with canned artichokes, goat cheese, and fresh herbs, and you've got the perfect stuffing for chicken. Or simply do them up with some cream cheese for your morning bagel.

Sun-dried tomatoes usually come dried or marinated in oil. Sun-dried tomatoes packed

VEAL SCALOPPINI WITH SUN-DRIED TOMATO SAUCE WITH ROASTED GARLIC AND WHITE WINE · POMME PURÉE · SAUTÉED RAPINI WITH GARLIC

Scaloppini refers to a thinly sliced piece of meat, usually veal, that has been breaded and pan-fried until golden brown. It's often served as an entrée with a wine- or tomato-based sauce, or sandwich-style in a bun.

Some Italian butchers invest great time and care in slicing their veal scaloppini, taking immense pride in how thin they can slice it. When super-thin slices are pan-fried, they become crispy and delicate. If the veal slices are too thick, the breading can burn while the veal is cooking through. The very best butchers

will slice the veal as you order it, knowing that pre-sliced scaloppini can dry out quickly.

I really love this sauce—it's strong and pungent and the sweet sun-dried tomatoes contrast beautifully with the salty anchovies. The sauce is nicely balanced with crisp white wine and freshly squeezed lemon.

The scaloppini and sauce are laid down on a cloud-like bed of Pomme Purée, with sautéed rapini. If you've never had rapini, get on board—it's tasty and immensely good for you. The best part is that it's excellent done up simply with a little garlic. *{Serves 4}*

VEAL SCALOPPINI WITH SUN-DRIED TOMATO SAUCE WITH ROASTED GARLIC AND WHITE WINE

Veal

four 3–4 oz veal cutlets
salt and pepper
1 cup flour
3 eggs, lightly beaten
1 cup breadcrumbs
½ cup grated Parmesan
3 Tbsp olive oil

Sun-dried tomato sauce

2 Tbsp olive oil
1 shallot, finely diced
2 anchovy fillets, finely chopped
½ cup julienned sun-dried tomatoes
1 small head roasted garlic
  (see page 73)
⅓ cup white wine
1 cup chicken stock
1 Tbsp butter
2 Tbsp lemon juice
salt and pepper

For the veal, season cutlets well with salt and pepper. Place flour in a large shallow dish. Place eggs in another large shallow dish. Combine breadcrumbs and Parmesan and place in a third large shallow dish. Dredge cutlets in flour, patting off excess, then dip into eggs, and finally, dredge in breadcrumbs. Heat 3 Tbsp olive oil in a large non-stick skillet over medium-high heat. Add cutlets to pan and sear sides until golden brown and cooked through, about 3 to 4 minutes per side (two batches may be necessary depending on size of pan). Place directly on the middle rack of a warm 200°F oven so scaloppini remains crispy.

For the sauce, wipe extra oil from veal pan, add 2 Tbsp olive oil and bring to medium heat. Gently fry shallot and anchovies, stirring until anchovies break down. Add sun-dried tomatoes and roasted garlic cloves; sauté for another minute. Deglaze with white wine and simmer to reduce slightly. Add chicken stock and bring back up to a simmer; reduce to sauce consistency. Lower heat and gently swirl in butter. Remove from heat, finish with lemon juice, and season with salt and pepper, if necessary. Keep sauce warm.

POMME PURÉE

2 lb potatoes (about 5 medium),
  peeled and quartered (Kennebec
  or russet potatoes are best)
1 bay leaf
salt
½ lb butter, cubed and at
  room temperature
¼ cup whipping cream (35%)

Place potatoes and bay leaf in a medium pot. Fill with cold water just to cover potatoes. Season cooking water well with salt (it should taste like the sea) and bring to a boil. Boil on medium-high heat until potatoes are tender but not overdone, about 10 to 15 minutes. Strain potatoes; let dry out slightly in colander.

Combine butter and whipping cream in a large saucepan over medium heat. When butter is melted and cream is hot, press potatoes through a ricer or food mill into the same saucepan. (If you don't have a ricer, simply add potatoes to the saucepan and mash well with a potato masher.) Gently fold potatoes and cream together. Season with salt. Keep warm.

SAUTÉED RAPINI WITH GARLIC

1 large bunch rapini
1 shallot, roughly sliced
2 Tbsp olive oil
1 small clove garlic, finely minced
salt and pepper

Bring a large pot of salted water to a rolling boil. Blanch rapini with shallot for about 2 minutes. Drain. Heat oil in a medium skillet over medium heat; add garlic and sweat without colouring. Add drained greens and sauté another 1 to 2 minutes. Season with salt and pepper.

TOMATOES

Tuh-MAY-toh or tuh-MAH-toh . . . it's up to you. Either way, tomatoes are an incredible fruit and their culinary uses are truly endless. They're amazing on their own and can be used in a multitude of recipes. There are over one thousand varieties of the popular fruit. The most common are red, yellow, and orange, but there are also pink, purple, green, and even white tomatoes. Tomatoes range in size, taste, and texture from small, sweet, tender cherry tomatoes to big, beautiful, juicy beefsteak tomatoes. Tomatoes are grown and enjoyed around the world; over 125 tons are produced globally every year.

When you're purchasing tomatoes, look for fruit

with a deep, rich colour. This is not only a sure sign of great taste, but also means that the tomato is loaded with health benefits like vitamins A and C, potassium, and iron. Good-quality tomatoes should be well shaped with smooth skin. Avoid fruit that has wrinkles, cracks, bruises, or soft spots. If a blemish-free tomato yields to slight pressure and has a noticeably fragrant and sweet aroma, it's ripe and ready to eat.

HEIRLOOM TOMATO PASTA BAKE WITH BLACK OLIVES AND RICOTTA · PANZANELLA SALAD WITH BUFFALO MOZZARELLA

Tomatoes are an absolutely essential aspect of Italian cuisine, and if there's one thing I've learned about making great Italian food, it's to keep it simple. This main is all about showcasing the natural tastes of simple, fresh, and beautiful ingredients. The hearty, delicious baked pasta, or *pasta al forno,* puts the texture and aroma of vine-ripened tomatoes front and centre. The nutty flavours of garlic and black pepper browned in olive oil and the sweet fragrance of gently fried basil complement the tomato's freshness perfectly. This easy and mouth-watering dish is a great make-ahead meal you can share with friends and family. *{Serves 4}*

HEIRLOOM TOMATO PASTA BAKE WITH BLACK OLIVES AND RICOTTA

1 lb bag rigatoni pasta

¼ cup olive oil

2 cloves garlic, crushed

6 basil leaves

1 tsp freshly ground black pepper

3 cups chopped yellow or
   orange tomatoes

1 tsp dried oregano

salt

½ cup grated Parmesan

¼ cup black olives, coarsely chopped

4–5 heirloom tomatoes, cut
   into wedges

1 cup fresh ricotta

good-quality extra virgin olive oil,
   for drizzling

6–8 fresh basil leaves, torn

Cook rigatoni in a large pot of salted water according to package directions. Remove from water when slightly undercooked, as pasta will continue to cook when baked.

In a large, deep saucepan, heat olive oil over medium heat. Add garlic and cook until light golden, 2 to 3 minutes. Add basil and pepper and let basil fry lightly in oil, about 1 minute. Add yellow or orange tomatoes and allow to cook down, about 10 to 15 minutes, or until tomatoes start to break down. The oil and tomato juice should emulsify to make a sauce. Crush tomatoes slightly, add oregano, and season with salt. Remove from heat.

Preheat oven to 375°F.

Add drained pasta to tomato sauce, stirring to combine. Add Parmesan and half of the olives. Stir to combine. Transfer pasta mixture to a 9- × 13-inch casserole dish.

Alternate heirloom tomato wedges and dollops of ricotta evenly on top of pasta. Sprinkle with remaining black olives. Drizzle with extra virgin olive oil. Bake for 20 to 30 minutes, or until golden and crusty on top. Remove from oven and sprinkle with fresh basil.

PANZANELLA SALAD WITH BUFFALO MOZZARELLA

½ loaf ciabatta bread (or any rustic
   loaf), cut into 1-inch cubes (about
   3 cups)

2 Tbsp olive oil

salt and black pepper

1½ cups olive oil

½ pint yellow grape or
   cherry tomatoes

½ pint red grape or cherry tomatoes

2 cloves garlic, crushed

5 basil leaves, plus extra for garnish

zest of 1 orange

pepper

⅓ cup diced red onion

¼ cup balsamic vinegar

pinch of salt

1 ball buffalo mozzarella, torn
   into pieces

sea salt and black pepper

Preheat oven to 400°F.

In a large bowl, toss bread with 2 Tbsp olive oil and salt and pepper. Spread onto a baking sheet and bake for 10 to 15 minutes, or until bread is golden brown.

In a medium saucepan, combine the 1½ cups of olive oil, half of the tomatoes, garlic, basil, and orange zest, and season with pepper. Set over low to medium heat and poach for 10 to 15 minutes, or until some skins start to break slightly. Remove from heat.

In a small bowl, combine red onion, balsamic vinegar, and a pinch of salt. Set aside.

To assemble, slice remaining fresh tomatoes in half. Divide cooked tomato mixture among 4 plates. Top with fresh tomatoes, red onion mixture, and buffalo mozzarella. Garnish with fresh basil leaves, reserved olive oil from poached tomato mixture, and sea salt and black pepper.

181

TROUT

There are many different varieties of trout in North America. The fish is usually found in very clean, cold water—lakes, rivers, and streams—which results in a nice delicate taste.

Rainbow trout, a freshwater variety, are primarily found in lakes. They are prized in the culinary world for their beautiful rainbow underbellies and delicate sweet flavour. Rainbow trout are available at most fishmongers and grocers. Because most varieties are small (2.5 to 4 pounds), they're often sold whole. When a fish is whole it's very easy to determine its freshness.

The eyes should be clear and bright and the gills should be vibrant red. The scales should be tight and unblemished by scrapes or cuts. The fish should also smell very clean and feel wet to the touch but not slimy.

Whole rainbow trout are absolutely delicious barbecued with herbs and spices, or cooked over an open fire. If you're looking for rainbow trout fillets, your fishmonger will be happy to fillet and skin the fish as well as remove the pin bones.

TROUT POT PIE WITH A CHIVE AND DILL BISCUIT CRUST · CLASSIC CAESAR SALAD

Fish pot pie is classic English country food. It's warm, comforting, hearty, and simple. I love how all the flavours and ingredients in this dish are commonplace and easy to work with and how they enhance the trout's subtle taste. The leeks have an onion and garlic flavour that complements delicate fishes. The carrots add a sweetness that plays nicely with that of the trout. Baking the fish in a creamy sauce under a crust of tender dill and chive biscuits keeps it deliciously moist and tender. If you can't find trout, use Arctic char or salmon.

A homemade caesar salad may not fit with the classic English theme, but who cares—the taste is hard to beat and the sharp, pungent, and acidic flavours are perfect with my trout pie. Salty and savoury, capers and anchovies are both quintessential components of a classic caesar. To top it off, you'll need lots of grated Parmesan.

This simple, heartwarming meal is based on years of experience and tradition—now that's a main! *{Serves 4}*

TROUT POT PIE WITH A CHIVE AND DILL BISCUIT CRUST

Veggie filling

2 large carrots, peeled and cut into
½-inch rounds
3 medium leeks, cleaned, sliced in
half, and cut into ½-inch pieces

Sauce

3 Tbsp butter
2½ Tbsp flour
½ cup white wine
2 cups milk
¼ cup chopped fresh dill
salt and pepper

Biscuit topping

1½ cups all-purpose flour
1 Tbsp baking powder
¾ tsp salt
½ cup cold butter, cut into
½-inch cubes
½ cup + 1 Tbsp whole milk
3 Tbsp chopped fresh dill
3 Tbsp chopped fresh chives
1 egg yolk mixed with 1 tsp water,
to make egg wash
coarse salt

Assembly

12 oz rainbow trout (or lake
trout) fillets
salt and pepper

To make the veggie filling, cover carrots with 2 inches of cold salted water in a medium pot. Bring to a boil and cook for 8 to 10 minutes. Add leeks and cook another 2 to 3 minutes, or until carrots and leeks are tender. Drain and set aside.

To make the sauce, melt butter in a medium saucepan over medium heat. Add flour and cook, stirring constantly, for about 1 to 2 minutes. Add white wine and stir to combine. Add milk, dill, and salt and pepper. Bring sauce to a boil, then simmer, stirring occasionally, about 4 minutes, or until slightly thickened. Remove pan from heat and set aside.

To make the biscuit topping, whisk together flour, baking powder, and salt in a medium bowl. Blend in butter cubes with your fingertips until the mixture resembles a coarse meal. Stir in milk and herbs with a fork until mixture just comes together.

Gather dough into a ball, then turn onto a lightly floured surface and knead 2 or 3 times. Roll out with a floured rolling pin into an 8-inch round, then cut out 4 biscuits, each slightly larger in diameter than a 2-cup ramekin.

Preheat oven to 450°F.

Cut the trout into 8 equal portions.

To assemble the pot pies, pour 3 Tbsp of prepared sauce into each of four 2-cup ramekins. Divide half of the leeks and carrots between the 4 ramekins. Put 1 portion of seasoned trout on top of vegetables and season with salt and pepper. Repeat layers: sauce, vegetables, trout.

Brush edge of ramekin with egg wash and place 1 biscuit over each ramekin. Brush entire biscuit with egg wash and sprinkle with coarse salt. Pierce each pot pie with a knife to allow steam to escape. Bake for 20 to 25 minutes, or until mixture is bubbling and biscuits are golden brown.

CLASSIC CAESAR SALAD

Croutons

1 Tbsp olive oil
1 clove garlic, crushed
3 slices country bread, cubed
salt and pepper

Dressing

1 small shallot, minced
2 Tbsp red wine vinegar
1½ Tbsp Dijon mustard
1 small garlic clove, minced
2 anchovy fillets, minced
1 tsp capers, finely chopped
1 tsp freshly ground black pepper
¼ cup olive oil

Assembly

6 cups torn romaine hearts
½ cup fresh shaved Parmesan

For the croutons, in a medium skillet, heat olive oil and garlic over medium-low heat. Add bread and toss in olive oil for 3 to 5 minutes, or until golden brown. Remove from heat and let cool to room temperature. Season with salt and pepper.

For the dressing, in a medium bowl, combine shallot, red wine vinegar, Dijon mustard, garlic, anchovies, capers, and black pepper. Whisk in olive oil in a slow, steady stream to emulsify dressing.

To assemble, in a large bowl, toss romaine hearts with dressing. Sprinkle with croutons and Parmesan shavings, and serve.

WHITE BEANS

"White bean" is a fairly loose term and can apply to any bean that is white (surprise, surprise). White beans have a straightforward taste, and like pasta, potatoes, and other simple ingredients, they make a great base, but it's important to bring loads of flavour to them. Cured meats like sausage,

bacon, or pancetta are great pairing options that enhance the subtle taste of white beans.

To cut down the cooking time of any dried beans or legumes, you can soak them in cold water in the fridge overnight. When it comes time to cook the beans, it's important not to season the liquid

they're cooked in until the last 10 to 20 minutes of cooking. Any salt will toughen their skin, making it virtually impossible for them to become tender.

A TRULY CLASSIC CASSOULET,
STRAIGHT FROM OLD-WORLD FRANCE

Cassoulet is quintessential French country fare from the Languedoc area. It's hearty, rustic, and simple, and I love that it's presented in its very own dish. It's a meal that warms the soul—the best kind of comfort food.

A cassoulet is similar to a stew or casserole. It's a combination of tender white beans, aromatics, and a rather hearty selection of meats, which can include sausage (multiple varieties), pork or bacon and confit, or roasted duck or goose. The real magic comes in blending all these delectable flavours and baking them together. Before a cassoulet goes into the oven, it is traditionally covered with herb-infused breadcrumbs. Once baked, this topping brings an amazing crunch, which contrasts nicely with the rest of the dish.

My version breaks from tradition slightly because I use merguez sausages. They're popular in France but more closely associated with Northern Africa. Regardless, this spicy, thin lamb sausage is one of my favourites, and its warm aromatic spice works exceptionally well with the rest of the ingredients in the cassoulet. {Serves 4}

A TRULY CLASSIC CASSOULET, STRAIGHT FROM OLD-WORLD FRANCE

White beans

2 cups dried white beans, soaked overnight
1 carrot, peeled and halved
1 small stalk celery
½ onion
3 garlic cloves, crushed
1 bay leaf

Drain soaked beans and rinse well. Put in a medium pot and cover with cold water. Add carrot, celery, onion, garlic, and bay leaf, and bring to a simmer. Skim any impurities that rise to the surface. Simmer gently until beans are just barely tender and cooked through, about 30 to 40 minutes. Strain, reserving liquid, and set aside.

Roasted duck and bacon

4 duck legs with thighs
2 Tbsp salt
1 Tbsp black pepper
4 pieces double smoked bacon, each about 1 inch thick and 3 inches long, rind trimmed
2 cloves garlic, crushed
2–3 sprigs thyme

Preheat oven to 450°F.
    Season duck legs well with salt and pepper. Arrange duck and bacon, fatty skin side up, in a large ovenproof casserole or deep baking dish. Add garlic and thyme. Fill with just enough water to cover up three-quarters of duck, so that skin remains above water level. Bake, uncovered, until skins are crispy and golden, about 40 to 45 minutes. Lower oven temperature to 350°F and bake another 25 to 30 minutes, or until duck is cooked and tender.

Base sauce

2 Tbsp olive oil
8 cloves garlic, crushed
1 medium carrot, diced
1 medium onion, diced
2 bay leaves
2 tsp pepper
¼ cup tomato paste
¼ cup duck fat (reserved from roasted duck and bacon recipe)
3 cups chicken stock
1 sprig thyme
1 sprig rosemary

Heat olive oil in a large heavy-bottomed pot over medium heat. Add crushed garlic and cook until light golden, about 1 or 2 minutes. Add carrot, onion, bay leaves, and pepper, and sauté gently until slightly coloured. Add tomato paste and *cook out* for a few minutes (see page 86). Add duck fat, chicken stock, thyme, and rosemary, and bring to a simmer. Set aside and keep warm.

Parsley breadcrumbs

2 cups roughly torn white baguette pieces (about ½ stick)
salt and pepper
¼ cup chopped parsley
¼ cup olive oil

Preheat oven to 350°F.
    Place baguette pieces on a baking sheet and season lightly with salt and pepper. Bake until golden brown and crispy, about 4 to 5 minutes. When cool enough to handle, roughly crush the bread, and add to bowl of a food processor. Add parsley and pulse to combine. Add olive oil in a stream; mixture should be crumbly and slightly moist.

Assembly

salt and pepper
1 Tbsp olive oil
4 merguez (or Barese) sausages

To assemble the cassoulet, add reserved strained beans to base sauce and continue to gently simmer for another 8 to 10 minutes. Adjust consistency with additional bean cooking liquid if mixture seems too dry. The bean mixture should be easy to stir, but not watery. Season with salt and pepper.
    In a separate pan, heat olive oil over medium-high heat. Brown sausages, whole, on all sides, until cooked through, about 5 to 7 minutes.
    Preheat oven to 450°F.
    Divide bean mixture evenly between 4 separate ovenproof bowls or small casserole dishes. Place sausages into bowls, followed by duck thighs and strips of bacon. Place thighs skin side up, so that skin shows through beans. Sprinkle parsley breadcrumbs over beans. Bake until beans are warmed through and bubbling and breadcrumbs are a deep golden brown, about 15 minutes.

189

YOGURT

Yogurt is a dairy product made through the fermentation of fresh milk. It is widely believed that yogurt, which originated in central Asia and Europe, was first made as many as 4,500 years ago. It was most likely discovered accidentally when nomads carrying fresh milk were surprised to find their supplies had curdled.

Yogurt is the best—thick, creamy, rich, and delicious. Take into account its legendary health benefits and super-versatility and you've got a seriously top-shelf ingredient! Yogurt not only promotes good health with high levels of potassium, protein, and vitamin B, it also provides endless possibilities in the kitchen.

It's a nutritious way to start the day, makes
a rich and healthy dessert, is a great addition to
baked goods and savoury dishes, and can also
be enjoyed in a multitude of drinks.

INDIAN-SPICED YOGURT-MARINATED CHICKEN · BLACK LENTILS · TOMATO CHUTNEY · SPICY CITRUS YOGURT

I'm using yogurt as the key player in an authentic Indian-inspired main: it serves as the base for a deliciously spicy and creamy sauce and also goes directly on the chicken alongside an enticing spice rub. This chicken is amazing enhanced with all the flavours in my Indian spice rub—no wonder spice combining is so highly respected in India! Once the chicken has marinated in the rub, add a layer of fresh, thick, and creamy yogurt. It's imperative to blend the spices on the outside of the chicken with the yogurt; it laces the meat with the most flavour possible, and the yogurt's natural tang cuts through the warmth of the spices and blends them together harmoniously. The acidity in the yogurt will also help to tenderize the chicken and keep it unbelievably moist as it cooks. My spicy yogurt sauce tops this main off perfectly. The heat from a few chilies combined with cool, creamy yogurt gives the sauce amazing contrast and brings all the components of the meal together. {Serves 4}

Marinate chicken in spices • Cook lentils and prepare tomato chutney • Add yogurt to chicken marinade • Cook shallots and curry leaves for lentils • Cook chicken • Finish lentils, tomato chutney, and spicy yogurt • Serve family-style with chutney and yogurt as condiments

INDIAN-SPICED YOGURT-MARINATED CHICKEN

2 Tbsp chopped cilantro stems
1 Tbsp grated ginger
juice of 1 lemon
2 cloves garlic, minced
1 Tbsp ground coriander seed
½ Tbsp paprika
¾ Tbsp ground cumin
1 tsp ground turmeric
1 tsp ground cardamom
1 tsp cayenne pepper
½ tsp cinnamon
½ tsp ground cloves
4 boneless, skinless chicken breasts
½ cup Greek-style (thick) yogurt
1 Tbsp vegetable oil
salt
1 Tbsp butter

In a medium bowl, mix cilantro stems, ginger, lemon juice, garlic, coriander, paprika, cumin, turmeric, cardamom, cayenne pepper, cinnamon, and cloves. Add chicken breasts and coat with marinade. Allow chicken to marinate in the refrigerator for at least 30 minutes and up to overnight.

Add yogurt to marinated chicken breasts, forming a paste with the spice mixture. Marinate another 20 minutes, or up to 2 hours in the refrigerator.

Preheat oven to 400°F.

In a large cast iron skillet, heat vegetable oil over medium-high heat. Season marinated chicken breasts with salt. Add chicken breasts to skillet. Sear until brown and slightly charred, about 3 minutes per side.

Add butter and transfer skillet to preheated oven. Cook until chicken is cooked through and tender, about 6 to 8 minutes more.

BLACK LENTILS

1½ cups black lentils, rinsed
1 Tbsp vegetable oil
2 small shallots, thinly sliced
¼ cup curry leaves
2 Tbsp butter
salt

In a large pot, bring 5 cups of salted water to a boil. Add lentils and cook for 15 to 20 minutes, or until tender. Drain lentils.

In a medium skillet, heat vegetable oil over medium heat. Add shallots and curry leaves and cook until shallots are golden brown and curry leaves are crackling, about 4 to 5 minutes. Add cooked lentils and stir to combine. Add butter and season with salt.

TOMATO CHUTNEY

1 Tbsp vegetable oil
1 small green chili, cut in half
½ tsp fennel seeds
½ tsp cumin seeds
4 medium tomatoes, coarsely chopped
2 sprigs cilantro, leaves only
juice of 1 lime

1½ Tbsp sugar
salt to taste
2 Tbsp chopped cilantro

In a medium skillet, heat vegetable oil over medium-high heat. Add chili, fennel seeds, and cumin seeds, and toast 2 to 3 minutes, or until fragrant.

Add tomatoes and cilantro leaves. Let mixture simmer for 10 to 15 minutes, or until thickened. Add lime juice and sugar, and season with salt. Remove from heat. When mixture has cooled, stir in cilantro.

SPICY CITRUS YOGURT

2 green chilies, seeded and
  finely chopped
1 red chili, seeded and
  finely chopped
zest of 1 lemon
zest of 1 lime
1 cup Greek-style (thick) yogurt
salt

In a medium bowl, combine green and red chilies, lemon and lime zests, and yogurt. Season with salt.

193

CONVERSION CHARTS

Volume		Weight		Temperature		Length	
¼ tsp	1 mL	2 oz	60 g	145°F	63°C	⅛ inch	3 mm
½ tsp	2 mL	4 oz	125 g	150°F	66°C	¼ inch	6 mm
¾ tsp	4 mL	¼ lb	125 g	200°F	95°C	⅓ inch	8 mm
1 tsp	5 mL	5 oz	150 g	250°F	120°C	½ inch	1 cm
½ Tbsp	7 mL	⅓ lb	170 g	300°F	150°C	¾ inch	2 cm
2 tsp	10 mL	6 oz	175 g	325°F	160°C	1 inch	2.5 cm
1 Tbsp	15 mL	8 oz	250 g	340°F	171°C	1½ inches	4 cm
¼ cup	60 mL	½ lb	250 g	350°F	180°C	2 inches	5 cm
⅓ cup	80 mL	10 oz	300 g	360°F	182°C	3 inches	8 cm
½ cup	125 mL	12 oz	375 g	375°F	190°C	4 inches	10 cm
⅔ cup	160 mL	¾ lb	375 g	400°F	200°C	8 inches	20 cm
¾ cup	185 mL	1 lb	500 g	425°F	220°C	9 inches	23 cm
1 cup	250 mL	1½ lb	750 g	450°F	230°C	10 inches	25 cm
2 cups	500 mL	2 lb	1 kg	475°F	240°C	13 inches	33 cm
3 cups	750 mL	3 lb	1.5 kg				
4 cups	1 L	4 lb	1.8 kg				
8 cups	2 L	5 lb	2.2 kg				

INDEX

194

197

198

ACKNOWLEDGEMENTS AND APPRECIATIONS

Thanks to:

My chefs:
Sylvain Cuerrier, Ollie Couillaud, and Steve Troung.

My friends at Food Network Canada:
Emily Morgan and Tanya Linton—for opening the door to my dreams and supporting me while I chase them. Holly Gillanders, Leslie Merklinger, Kathy Cross, and Lesley Birchard—for the constant encouragement and inspiration.

The judges of Superstar Chef Challenge II:
Michael Smith, Christine Cushing, Dominic Cyriax—I wouldn't be here without you.

The Main team:
Jennifer Fraser ("J-Rock"), Ellen Heron Howell ("Dr" to me, "Dr. Howell" to the rest), Claudia Bianchi ("C"), who was on the scene right from the get-go, Justin Courneya ("Juicy"), Marc Simard ("Marks and Sparks" to me, "Knuckle Meat" to many), Jeff Baker, Jane Van Deuren ("J"), Eva Filomena ("E", "Easy E," or "Eva Longoria"), Flo Leung, Brent Martin ("B Roll"), Kyle Woodley ("K-Mart"), Ben Sharp ("B-Bombs") and his team, for constantly taking the piss out of me. You, sir, have the kitchen spirit. To everyone else who is behind the scenes long before I arrive, and long after I go home—thank you.

And, finally, to *David Bagosy* for the incredible food shots, and for making me look good.